Employers Large
and Small

Employers Large and Small

Charles Brown, James Hamilton,
and James Medoff

Harvard University Press
Cambridge, Massachusetts
London, England
1990

Library of Congress Cataloging in Publication Data
Brown, Charles, 1949–
Employers large and small / Charles Brown, James Hamilton, and James Medoff.
p. cm.
Includes bibliographical references.
ISBN 0-674-25162-8
1. Employees—United States. 2. Small business—United States—Employees.
3. Big business—United States—Employees.
4. Industries, Size of—United States. 5. Wages—United States.
6. Employee fringe benefits—United States. I. Hamilton, James,
1961– . II. Medoff, James L., 1947– . III. Title.
HD5724.B725 1990   89-20080
331.2′973—dc20   CIP

To our families

Acknowledgments

We are indebted to the following people for their help in our research: Susan Bourneuf, Maryellen Driscoll, Brian Guthrie, Cheryl Hansen, Jennifer Hersch, Michael Horvath, Nancy Lemrow, Marsha Silverberg, William Stevens, and David Weil. Martin VanDenburgh provided able computer assistance, and Skipper Hammond did an excellent job in typing the manuscript. We appreciate the suggestions offered by Michael Aronson of Harvard University Press. Portions of our research were supported by the National Science Foundation (Grant no. 2342) and the Small Business Administration (Contract no. SBA 2104-AER-87).

Contents

Employers Large
and Small

· 1 ·

Images of Large and Small Employers

We have lived through the age of big industry and the
age of the giant corporation. But I believe that this is the
age of the entrepreneur.

—Ronald Reagan, 1985

The 1980s may well be remembered as the age of the entrepreneur. Figures such as the founders of high-tech firms were lionized as the new generation of American business leaders. Small firms were seen as the source of change in the economy, offering new jobs, new ideas, and new ways of treating their employees, and large firms were viewed as a brake on growth, firing workers, becoming less competitive abroad, and turning more and more to the government for help in reversing their fortunes. The much-heralded growth of the service sector and the painful slide of manufacturing industries confirmed that the future lay in small businesses. This image of small firms as both beautiful and bountiful is an appealing one, but it needs to be both reexamined and expanded.

The prevailing wisdom about large and small firms should be reexamined because in at least two instances, job creation and political power, it is wrong. Perhaps the most widespread misconception about small businesses in the United States is that they generate the vast majority of jobs and are therefore the key to economic growth. Our research, however, shows that small businesses do not create as many jobs as advocates claim and that differences in the job creation rates of large and small firms have few policy implications in any case. Overall the economy is not becoming more dependent on smaller firms for employment: the proportion of workers employed in small firms in 1986 was not very different from (and if anything was *smaller* than) the proportion in 1958.

Another mistaken belief about small businesses is that they lack political power. Many debates over policies affecting small firms are interspersed with claims that these "mom-and-pop" enterprises lack influence in Washington. Yet the evidence demonstrates that small business possesses considerable political resources in terms of political contributions, staff, and favorable public opinion.

Most discussions contrasting the economic contributions of large and small firms focus on job creation. But there are many other aspects of economic conduct and performance to consider. Businesses do more than simply create jobs. They sell products, do research, structure wage and benefit agreements, control their employees' work environment, and interact with government. Much is known about some of these aspects of firm behavior. Labor economists have known for a long time that there is a sizable difference in the wages and benefits enjoyed by employees in large firms and by their counterparts in small firms. Regulatory economists have studied how the exemptions in government regulations and standards of enforcement vary by firm size. Political observers have long remarked on the power of small business lobbies to influence the course of legislation in Congress. Yet these facts have not resulted in a clear and complete picture in the minds of the public or policymakers of the differences between large and small firms.

The following pages focus on eight elements to create a fuller picture of the role of large and small employers in the economy. We focus primarily on large and small firms in their role as *employers* because we feel that it is the area most in need of deeper examination. We do not attempt to discover partisan points for one interest or the other. Rather we intend the book to be an empirical collage which creates a picture more complete than the current conceptions of large and small employers. The main elements of our picture are:

1. Small employers do not create a particularly impressive share of jobs in the economy, especially when we focus on jobs that are not short-lived. Policymakers and small business advocates invariably cite the work of David Birch, who in a 1981 article for the *Public Interest* concluded that between 1969 and 1976 "small buinesses" created eight out of ten new jobs (Birch, 1981). The trouble is that Birch generally defined business size by the number of people working at a given location rather than by the number working for the firm in total—a technique that means that when a new Sears outlet opens, its 75 employees would be counted as evidence of "small business growth" rather than as evidence of expansion by a large employer. In contrast, a Small Business Administration (SBA) study of the same period that took into account total firm size found that firms with fewer than 100 workers accounted for only 56 percent of new jobs (SBA, 1983). Small firms' share of new jobs is also quite sensitive to

the period studied. Moreover, if short-lived jobs are excluded, the higher failure rates for small businesses make the share of nontransitory jobs generated by small employers even lower.

Although subsequent research has revised estimates of job generation power of small business downward, the early figures continue to live on in policy circles. Thus U.S. Chamber of Commerce president Richard Lesher asserted in 1986: "Small business is America's ace-in-the-hole. Small businesses create eight out of every ten new jobs" ("Small Business in America," 1986, p. S19). And in announcing a state program to support small business, Governor James Thompson of Illinois declared that small buinesses are "where the jobs are going to come from" (Lublin, 1984, p. 33).

2. Large employers offer much higher wages than small employers, even when differences in employees' education and experience and the nature of the industry are considered. In 1983 the average wage of workers in large firms was 35 percent higher than that of their counterparts in small ones.

3. Large employers also offer better benefits. For example, 83 percent of nonunion firms with 500 or more employees offer pension plans, compared with 33 percent of smaller firms. In addition, almost all large firms offer life, health, and accident insurance, compared with two-thirds of small ones.

4. The lower level of fringe benefits offered by small firms is due at least in part to higher per-employee costs of some fringes. Small employers also pay more when they borrow money to invest and when they buy other non-labor inputs.

5. The reason large employers offer higher compensation is *not* because they offer inferior working conditions. In fact, when working conditions are taken into account, large employers still pay more than their smaller counterparts. In addition, various indicators of employees' satisfaction with the work environment do not indicate that conditions are more favorable in small firms. Statutory exemptions of small firms from some government regulations concerning working conditions and lax enforcement of others leave workers in these firms less protected than their counterparts in larger firms with no *de jure* or de facto exemptions. While particular regulations are sometimes more costly for small firms than for larger ones, often this is because small firms are less likely to engage in the behavior the regulation is meant to require; for example, minimum-wage increases are more costly to small businesses because small firms are more likely to be paying low wages in the first place.

6. The jobs generated by large employers provide greater, not less, security than those generated by small employers. Layoff rates, which reflect all kinds of layoffs, are much lower in large businesses than in comparable small ones.

7. The owners of small firms enjoy incomes and assets higher than those of the average American. When the assets and income of families that own small businesses are compared with those of the average family, the true direction of the redistribution of income from small business favoritism becomes clear. According to our tabulations from the University of Michigan's 1983 Survey of Consumer Finances, families who owned small businesses had incomes that were 1.8 times higher than the income of the average U.S. family and owned assets that were more than five times as large. Alternatively, if we compare ownership of small business to ownership of large firms through stock ownership, small businesses are owned by households with lower incomes but about the same level of wealth as are large ones. It is important to recognize, however, that the typical small business owner has a relatively large share of his or her wealth tied up in that business, and so the small business owner's wealth is very vulnerable to downside risk for the business. Given the failure rate of small businesses, that downside risk is probably quite severe.

8. Small employers do possess significant political resources in terms of PAC dollars, lobbying staff, and public support, even in comparison with those of labor and large employers. In the 1984 U.S. Senate campaigns, for example, small business PACs accounted for 23 percent of incumbents' total PAC contributions. Making the connection between votes and contributions even clearer, the National Federation of Independent Business (NFIB) offers potential PAC support (and its Guardian of Small Business Award) to all legislators who score at least 70 percent on its rating of congressional votes—and guarantees potential support for the challenger to any legislator who scores less than 40 percent. As a lobbyist for NFIB put it in assessing the impact of these political resources: "Small business is a terrifically effective lobbying force. There are more of us. Our members are personally involved in their businesses; they aren't managers. Our people make up the vast majority of the moderate-to-conservative, politically active people back home" (Matlack, 1987, p. 2596).

Each of these eight points will be viewed as obvious to some observers and suspect by others. Taken as a whole, they paint a more complete picture of large and small employers than the view that focuses primarily on small business's power to create jobs and inability to contend in politics.

Developing a truer picture of large and small employers is important because current programs to aid small firms and to exempt them from regulations may in part be based on incorrect and incomplete knowledge. Before we go on to develop this picture of large and small employers, we briefly examine why the previous view has held sway for so long. Are the points we weave together not fully appreciated because the trends examined are new? Or are people predisposed *not* to believe results which might run contrary to an ingrained sympathy for "small" institutions?

The economic and political differences we highlight between large and small employers do not appear to be a new phenomenon. Trends in job generation by firm size are hard to extend back in time, for the data base on firm births and deaths used by most researchers in the field has only been analyzed back to 1969. Yet broader evidence does dispel the notion that the economy is becoming more dependent on small employers. Piecing together trends from two data sources with three different conventions about industrial coverage, it appears that the share of employment accounted for by firms with fewer than 500 workers fell between 1958 and 1962, and has not shown much trend since then. The share of sales accounted for by small firms is also declining, from 57 percent in 1958 to 50 percent in 1982 (SBA, 1987). (Small firms' share of sales is measured in terms of the "gross product originating" in small firms.)

The available evidence also indicates that results such as higher pay for workers in larger firms are not just a recent experience, though historical data once again do not permit as extensive analysis as modern figures. Wage information collected by the government in the 1890 Census of Manufactures shows that men who worked in larger manufacturing firms earned higher pay than their counterparts in small firms (Goldin, 1986). A report by the Bureau of Labor Statistics in 1940 found further evidence of the historical persistence of this pay pattern. The Bureau's study of wage scales during the latter years of the 1930s was prepared for a special Senate Committee created in the wake of the Depression to conduct an "Investigation of Concentration of Economic Power." Though the investigation focused on the dangers of growing concentration of markets among large corporations, the section on wages pointed out: "One important question has rarely been raised: Is the growth of 'big business' beneficial to workers, as measured by earnings?" (Bureau of Labor Statistics, 1940, p. xiii). The report concluded that it was, for it found that "the workers in plants of big companies have higher earnings than those in small companies" (p. xi).

The successful exercise of political power by small businesses is also not a new phenomenon. Even at the height of the Gilded Age, the passage and interpretation of a string of antitrust laws, beginning with the Sherman Act of 1890, reflected in part a populist desire to protect small business. As Judge Learned Hand acknowledged in the *Alcoa* case,

> In the debate in Congress Senator Sherman himself . . . showed that among the purposes of Congress in 1890 was a desire to put an end to great aggregations of capital because of the helplessness of the individual before them . . . Throughout the history of these statutes it has been constantly assumed that one of their purposes was to perpetuate and preserve, for its own sake and in spite of possible cost, an organization of industry in small units . . . (Posner, 1981, p. 614)

The battles between big and small business interests such as those in retailing did not end with the nineteenth century. As chain stores gained market share during the 1920s and 1930s, hard-pressed mom-and-pop retailers sought legislative protection from competition with larger stores.[1] Almost half the states passed tax laws to hinder the spread of chain stores, typically by setting a license fee per store that increased with the number of stores in the state operated by the chain. In 1936 the Robinson-Patman Act attempted to protect small businesses nationwide by restricting suppliers' use of discounts to larger buyers. During World War II Congress enacted the Small Business Act of 1942 and created the Smaller War Plants Corporation, which provided small businesses with government assistance and encouraged the use of small firms in production for the war effort. In 1953 Congress created the Small Business Administration "to aid, counsel, assist and protect, insofar as is possible, the interests of small business," a mission that it pursues to this day.

Since the economic and political trends we examine about large and small employers are not new, then why have they failed to become part of the currently accepted picture of small and large firms? A large part of the answer probably lies in Americans' predisposition to favor small business and distrust large firms. Big business often elicits the same reaction as big government in the minds of policymakers and the public. Both conjure up images of large institutions that, despite worthwhile stated goals, have grown unmanageable and unresponsive. Part of this distrust stems from Americans' ingrained hostility toward large organizations of any type. Whether it is the Jeffersonian ideal of agrarian democracy in the early 1800s, the Progressive Era of trustbusting and the protection of the small businessman in the early 1900s, or the popularization of E. F. Schumacher's notion that "small is beautiful" in the 1970s, Americans have often idealized and elevated institutions perceived as "small." As Seymour Martin Lipset and William Schneider put it, "Whenever surveys have dealt with different size levels of the same institution, they have found greater hostility to the 'big' or 'large' versions than to smaller ones" (Lipset and Schneider, 1987, p. 80). Thus, in a Gallup survey in 1975, only 35 percent of respondents had a great deal of confidence in "large" companies, compared with 57 percent who said they had a great deal of confidence in "small" companies (ibid., p. 72). Among journalists the distrust is even greater: in a 1984 survey of working journalists, 80 percent rated the credibility of small business proprietors as good or excellent, but only 53 percent rated the credibility of chief executive officers of corporations as highly (Opinion Research Corporation, 1984).

Public support for small business spills over into the political sphere. When asked whether "small businesses should have less government regulation than large businesses," 56 percent of a sample of adults agreed they should, as did a large majority of small business owners and managers (Chilton, 1984). Finally, a survey of general public attitudes toward entrepreneurial and small business found a strong belief that small business owners had too little political influence in America while corporate executives had too much (Jackson, 1986).

Programs to aid small firms may thus stem from an overwhelming populist strain in American politics. The goal of helping small employers may also be part of many sound public policies such as general programs to encourage economic development among businesses of all sizes or particular programs to correct market failures especially detrimental to small firms. However, to the extent that these policies are based on widely-held beliefs about small business job generation, political impotence, or redistribution to the disadvantaged, they will be based on fiction, not truth. As one researcher at the Brookings Institution has pointed out, the popular conceptions about small business have led to an "Eleventh Commandment" in politics: "Thou shalt aid and protect small business because it creates jobs" (Richman, 1983, p. 64).

How many jobs do small employers really create, what kind of jobs are they, and how long do they last? These are among the questions we explore in the following chapters to build a fuller, more accurate picture of the sizable differences between large and small employers in our society.

· 2 ·

The Economic Backdrop

> The good health and strength of America's small busi-
> nesses are a vital key in the health and strength of our
> economy . . . indeed, small business is America.
>
> —Ronald Reagan, 1984

Although for many people the terms *big business* and *small business* evoke ready images of large, bureaucratic enterprises or small, mom-and-pop corner stores, there is no set definition of the size boundaries that make a business large or small. Many of the firms that people associate with big business, such as law firms and investment companies, are small in terms of number of employees. Law firms such as Coudert Brothers (with clients such as ABC, Atlantic Richfield, Citibank, Ford, NBC, and Xerox) or Hughes, Hubbard, and Reed (with very large clients such as Beatrice, McDonald's, Northwest Air, and Pepsi) and investment firms such as Kohlberg, Kravis, Roberts have fewer than 500 employees. Firms such as Chrysler or Northwest Airlines may be classified as large on the basis of their sales or number of employees, yet within their industries they are sometimes considered small. Members of the professions are seldom associated with the small business image of a neighborhood grocer or a local restaurant. Yet doctors and lawyers often practice in solo offices or in small partnerships. The average firm size for doctors is 11, for lawyers 16 (SBA, 1986b). The relative meaning of "big" and "small" thus depends on the question asked and the measure of size used.

The federal government's own definitions of small business vary by industry, and sometimes also by the agency doing the defining. Some measures of size are based on the number of workers, some on the size of sales or assets. The definition used most frequently by the government, however, appears to be the one employed by the Small Business Administration in its annual report *The State of Small Business*, in which a small business is one that employs fewer than 500 workers.

In the following pages we generally use the SBA definition, classifying firms with 500 or more workers as "big business" and those with fewer than 500 as "small business." Evidence about location size, which refers to the size of the actual workplace (such as a plant or establishment) is sometimes presented when the phenomenon under examination relates to workplace size or when data on firm size are not readily available. Small locations are generally defined here as those workplaces that employ fewer than 100 people. Although the precise cutoffs for the inclusion of a firm in the "big business" or "small business" category may be debated, the measures of size are highly correlated so that the choice of the large firm cutoff does not affect our results or conclusions in any qualitative sense. Our conclusions are the same when the large-small employer divide is set at 100 employees as when it is set at 500.

Small and Large Roles

The overwhelming majority of businesses in the United States are small businesses. Of an estimated 18.1 million nonfarm business tax returns filed in 1987, 12.6 million were sole proprietorships and 1.9 million were partnerships (SBA, 1988). Fewer than 7,000 of these companies employed more than 500 workers. Sales figures, however, may provide a more meaningful measure of the role of big and small business in the economy. As Table 2–1 shows, the share of sales of firms with fewer than 500 employees varies significantly by industry, ranging from a high of 88 percent in agriculture, forestry, and fishing to a low of 15 percent in manufacturing. Sales figures also provide a benchmark for measuring whether the economy is growing "more dependent" on small firms. In its review of the changing patterns of the size and composition of the U.S. economy, the SBA found that the share of total sales by small firms shrank from 57 percent in 1958 to 52 percent in 1977. By 1982 the share of total sales by small firms had fallen to 50 percent.[1] Hence, at least by this measure, the economy is growing less, not more, dependent on small businesses.

Participation in the government procurement market and research and development (R&D) efforts are two other measures often used to assess the role of small business in the economy. Of the $200 billion the government spent on private goods and services in 1986, small businesses supplied $36.3 billion (18 percent) directly and an additional $24.3 billion through subcontracts with larger firms (SBA, 1988). Comparing the roles of small and large firms in R&D (and innovativeness more generally) is

Table 2-1. Percentage of sales by small businesses, by industry, 1982

Industry	Firms with fewer than 100 employees	Firms with fewer than 500 employees
All industries	33	44
Agriculture, forestry, and fishing	75	88
Mining	13	19
Construction	64	78
Manufacturing	11	15
Transportation, communications, and public utilities	18	26
Wholesale trade	63	79
Retail trade	47	56
Finance, insurance, and real estate	37	52
Services	39	55

Source: Small Business Administration, 1986, p. 30.

less straightforward. Those who emphasize the innovative role of small firms tend to stress the lack of bureaucracy, which sometimes leads large firms to overlook the potential of their researchers' ideas. Moreover, if a new firm is created to exploit an idea for a new product or process, it is likely to be small, at least at first, because new businesses in general tend to be small. On the other hand, large businesses have advantages when innovation requires (or benefits from) a relatively large corps of researchers working on different aspects of a potential innovation. Moreover, older, more mature firms are less likely to be constantly threatened with failing altogether, and may therefore be better able to afford the sustained effort that some innovations require.

Where are significant innovations more likely to emerge: in the garage of Steve Jobs, where the Apple computer was conceived, or in the corporate labs of IBM, a current center of superconductivity research? To date, economic research on R&D has found no conclusive evidence that a firm's size affects its success in R&D.[2] A National Science Foundation study concluded that small businesses are more likely to spend R&D funds on basic research, whereas large ones concentrate more on product development and production (SBA, 1987). But a study of technological innovation using data from the Federal Trade Commission found that, among businesses that conduct R&D, firm size explains only a very small fraction of the differences in R&D intensity (Cohen, Levin, and Mowery, 1987).

One study looking at 635 product innovations in the 1970s found that small companies produced 2.5 times as many innovations per employee as large ones (SBA, 1983). Another study of 8,000 innovations recorded in 1982 also found a higher innovation/worker ratio in smaller firms (Acs and Audretsch, 1988). (A curious finding of this study was that the higher the share of industry employment in large firms, the greater the share of innovation in an industry by small firms.) Thus, it appears that small firms do generate a greater share of innovations than their share of employment might suggest. What is less clear is how to interpret this finding: Do new ideas lead to the creation of new firms (which are typically small when the innovation is first recorded), or do established small firms out-innovate large ones?

Since one of the prime concerns of our research is the relative advantages of working for large or small employers, a key statistic is the share of the workforce employed in firms of different sizes. Roughly half (46 percent) of the workforce is employed by firms with fewer than 500 workers; a roughly similar fraction (56 percent) work at establishments with fewer than 100 workers. Not surprisingly, employment in large firms is concentrated in larger workplaces (see Table 2–2). In firms with fewer than 500 employees, 87 percent of the workers are employed in locations with fewer than 100 people, whereas in firms with 500 or more employees only 30 percent are employed in locations with fewer than 100. This concentration of large firms' workers in large workplaces is important for at least two reasons. First, exemptions from government regulation often are defined by rules that exempt small workplaces, which because of the concentration of small business workers in small locations means these workers are less likely to be covered by regulation. Second, because large companies tend to have large workplaces and small companies small ones,

Table 2–2. Distribution of company employment by location size, 1983 (percentages)

	Firms with fewer than 500 employees	Firms with 500 or more employees
Percent of workers in locations with:		
Fewer than 100 employees	87	30
100 or more employees	13	70

Source: Bureau of Labor Statistics, May 1983 Current Population Survey.

even when data are available only about workplace size we can make inferences about companies of different sizes.

Although total employment is split about 50/50 between small and large firms, employment ratios vary significantly by industry. As Table 2–3 reveals, agriculture, forestry, and fishing; construction; wholesale trade; and retail trade are all industries in which the majority of the workers are employed by small employers. By contrast, in manufacturing; transportation, communications, and public utilities; and mining the majority work in firms that employ 500 or more. Thus, at a minimum business cycles and the restructuring of individual industries will affect workers in big and small business differently.

Not only are there important differences in the proportions of large and small firms in different industries; there is also an incredible variety even within industries that are quite narrowly defined. For example, one-fifth of those employed in highway and street construction work for firms with fewer than 20 employees, while another fifth are employed by businesses with 500 or more workers. Ten percent of those canning fruits and vegetables work for companies with fewer than 100 employees, but half work for firms with more than 10,000. One-third of those who make children's outerwear do so in firms with fewer than 100 workers, but another third work in firms more than ten times that large. This variety allows us to check whether differences between employers of different sizes hold for

Table 2–3. Percentage of employment in small businesses, by industry, 1982

Industry	Firms with fewer than 100 employees	Firms with fewer than 500 employees
All industries	32	46
Agriculture, forestry, and fishing	65	85
Mining	21	42
Construction	65	80
Manufacturing	16	26
Transportation, communications, and public utilities	21	31
Wholesale trade	57	85
Retail trade	50	60
Finance, insurance, and real estate	32	47
Services	29	49

Source: Small Business Administration, 1986, p. 30.

firms of different sizes in the same industry (that is, to control statistically for industry).

The Whys of Size

The existence of important differences in the size of the "typical" firm across industries, along with considerable variation within industries, leads to an obvious question: Why? The best size for a firm reflects a balance between forces that make it desirable for the firm to be larger and those that make larger size undesirable. If this were not the case, we should expect all firms to be either tiny or enormous—and we know this is not so.

One of the more obvious factors making large-scale operation profitable is that, at least up to a point, larger-scale production can allow firms to increase output with a less-than-proportional increase in the resources devoted to production. In particular, it is often possible to increase output without increasing expenditures for machinery and other capital proportionally (Scherer, 1980). Sometimes this is a reflection of basic geometry: doubling the capacity of a factory or shopping mall requires doubling the amount of land on which it is built, but each wall needs to be only about 40 percent longer. Another tendency toward economies of scale reflects the fact that, organizational problems aside, it is always possible to buy two machines if the smaller one is efficient (scale up) but not to buy half of a bigger machine that is more efficient. Manufacturing more of a given product makes it cost effective for managers to spend time to work out "minor" flaws in the organization of production, since the benefits of doing so are larger. Finally, larger-scale operation makes it possible for workers to specialize, learning to do fewer jobs better.

A variety of evidence suggests that although these advantages of larger production can be important, eventually they tend to become unimportant. The most often-cited disadvantage of a firm's becoming too large is that large organizations become too difficult to coordinate and manage effectively. Every business has only one chief executive, and growth forces that individual to coordinate more and more functions directly or indirectly through subordinates, from which he or she becomes more remote. In addition to coordinating workers' activities, firms must monitor them: learning who is working productively is essential to sensible pay, promotion, and dismissal decisions (Rosen, 1982; Oi, 1983). The owner of a small business can observe every employee daily; the personnel department of a large firm must make sense of a stack of rating forms filled out by supervisors with inevitably different rating standards (Stigler, 1962).

Production costs depend on prices paid for inputs and on how effectively those inputs are used. As we discuss in more detail in Chapter 4, small firms pay less for their labor, but they pay higher interest rates on borrowed funds and higher prices for intermediate inputs (such as raw materials and office supplies).

These factors do much to explain why the average dry-cleaning business is smaller than the average automobile manufacturer, and why the "typical" firm in many industries is neither huge nor tiny. But they do not provide a very satisfactory explanation for why firms of very different sizes exist in the same industry. Several additional factors are likely to be important here.

First, firms in the same industry, even when "industry" is narrowly defined, produce quite different products. Often large businesses concentrate on mass-produced, standardized goods while smaller ones produce small-batch, customized goods for which there are few advantages of scale (Oi, 1983).

Differences in demand for competing but nonidentical products can also explain differences in scale of operations. Even though the production processes for different beers may be similar, firm size would be expected to differ to the extent that consumers in the aggregate want more of one firm's beer than of another's. The size of the market is likely to be a particularly important constraint on firm size when goods are produced for local rather than national markets.

Third, differences in managers' or owners' ability to manage large organizations may contribute to variation in firm size. With sufficient competition in the market for managers, those able to run larger operations will command higher salaries, but different-sized firms (managed by people with different levels of ability to deal with size) can coexist in the same industry (Rosen, 1982; Oi, 1983).

Fourth, businesses do not decide they want to be a certain size and attain that size immediately. Rather, they are born small and (if they are lucky) grow gradually. Well-publicized examples such as Genetech to the contrary, capital markets are not eager to finance rapid expansion of unproven enterprises. It may also be more expensive to train workers and to match them to positions when the organization is growing rapidly (Prescott and Visscher, 1980). Thus, a distribution of firm sizes is to be expected if only because older ones are likely to be further along in the process of growth.

Workers and Owners

Table 2–4 also reveals that the demographics of workforces differ markedly with firm size. Large employers hire workers with more education (they have 9 percent fewer employees with less than a high school diploma and 7 percent more who have gone beyond high school). The workers in large businesses are also on average older (firms with 500 or more employees have a higher percentage of workers over age twenty-five than do small firms). Women are also more likely to end up working for small employers: 41 percent of the big business workforce is female, versus 46 percent for small business. This difference only partially reflects the concentration of women in industries dominated by small business. Another salient demographic difference between big and small business is the extent of unionization: 10 percent of workers in firms with fewer than 500 employees are unionized, versus 30 percent of workers in larger firms. Since the work environment is very different in unionized versus nonunion firms, we will often take unionization into account when we analyze the differences between large and small firms.

Owners of small and large businesses differ just as their employees do, and direct comparison is very difficult. Nevertheless, the existing data imply that owners of small firms are no poorer than owners of large firms. Probably the best source of information is the 1983 Survey of Consumer Finances (Curtin, Juster, and Morgan, forthcoming), which includes data on income, net worth, and two assets of particular interest: common stock and mutual fund shares in publicly traded corporations, and the value (net of related debts) of equity in farms and businesses (including partnerships and closely held corporations). Apart from the omission of ownership of corporate stock through pension funds, the first asset category corresponds reasonably well to ownership of large firms. The second corresponds tolerably well to ownership of small business, since respondents reported a management interest in 80 percent of the farm and business equity in question. When ownership of small and large businesses is com-

Table 2–4. Characteristics of large and small employer workforces, 1983
(percentages)

Characteristic	Employers with fewer than 500 workers	Employers with 500 or more workers
Sex		
Male	54	59
Female	46	41
Age		
Under 25	26	18
25–44	48	55
45–54	13	15
55 or over	12	12
Race		
White	90	89
Nonwhite	10	11
Education		
Less than high school diploma	22	13
High school diploma only	42	43
More than high school diploma	37	44
Union coverage		
Covered	10	30
Not covered	90	70
Industry		
Mining	1	2
Construction	9	2
Manufacturing	17	38
Transportation, commu-nications, and other public utilities	4	11
Wholesale and retail trade	29	21
Finance, insurance, and real estate	6	9
Services	34	17

Source: Bureau of Labor Statistics, May 1983 Current Population Survey.

pared in terms of overall net worth, the patterns are broadly similar. The least wealthy 90 percent of households owned about 10 percent of each type of business. Those with net assets between $250,000 and $500,000 owned 15 percent of large firms and only 8 percent of small firms. Those with assets of $500,000 or more owned 75 percent of big firms and 80 percent of small ones. Given that some "closely held corporations" are counted here (incorrectly) as small businesses, it is unwise to make much of these differences.

When households are ranked by income rather than by wealth, owners of small business do seem less well-to-do: the 2 percent of households with the highest incomes owned 70 percent of the large firms, compared with 45 percent of the smaller ones. However, reporting of income by small business owners is somewhat problematic (in particular, increased value of the business is unlikely to be counted), so that the results tend to show them as less well-to-do.

Thus, the existing, far from ideal data suggest that owners of small businesses are somewhat wealthier but report somewhat lower incomes than owners of stock in larger firms. What is quite clear is that owners of businesses of any size are a good deal wealthier than the rest of the population.

Generating New Jobs

I urge the Congress to listen to the small business owners who have increased overall employment so dramatically . . . It cannot be presumed that this national
resource—small business—can continue to flourish as it
has in the past if it is overly burdened with mandates or
obligations or with excessive taxation and regulation.

—Ronald Reagan, 1988

As you all know, small business creates about 80 percent
of the jobs in this country.

—Senator Dale Bumpers

Everybody *does* know [that small business creates 80
percent of new jobs] since it is invoked to justify small-
business demands for kinder treatment by government.
What they probably *don't* know is that it is misleading at
best and flat wrong at worst.

—*Wall Street Journal* reporters
David Wessel and Buck Brown, Nov. 8, 1988

Until the past decade, the stability of large firms' market shares and the
emphasis on slow-to-change determinants of market structure such as
economies of scale seemed to justify treating changes in firm size as grad-
ual and, for some purposes, ignorable. Although the behavior of large
firms remains an important issue, new evidence has suggested that within
this framework of relative stability in employment there is a rapid and
disorderly birth, growth, shrinkage, and disappearance of businesses at
largely offsetting rates. Small businesses are often portrayed as playing a
disproportionate role in this picture of micro instability underlying macro-
stability. They are seen as generating a disproportionate share of new
jobs; their dynamism is contrasted to the much less impressive job creation of larger firms.

As the quotations that begin this chapter suggest, this dynamic role is
seen as having profound policy implications. If job growth is an important

national goal (because concern about inflation leads policymakers to settle for higher unemployment than is otherwise desirable), and if small businesses are the source of most new jobs, it follows (it is argued) that the impact of regulations and other policies on these tiny job generators deserves special attention.

However, if the facts are simply that new jobs are generated by new firms, which tend to be small, but that small firms are *not* becoming more important sources of employment, then policy decisions to make special allowances for small business are misguided. We will argue that many of the beliefs about job generation that greatly condition policy are inconsistent with the facts.

Dynamics of Job Generation

Much of the emphasis on the dynamics of job generation has been a response to availability of data on individual businesses over time: the Small Business Administration has assembled a data base derived primarily from Dun and Bradstreet's file of firms attempting to establish credit or interacting with other businesses seeking credit information. Like other sources of data on firms (such as the Census Bureau's census of business), this file misses some firms, particularly new and very small ones. Nevertheless, it "covers approximately 93 percent of full-time business activity, generally firms with at least one paid employee, with a Dun and Bradstreet credit rating, or using insurance markets" (SBA, 1988a, p. 15).

For our purposes, the data have two important features: first, they allow us to follow firms over time, including new firms; second, employment is measured at the company as well as the establishment level. This is important because there is evidence that new or small establishments owned by large firms play an important role in generating jobs (Armington and Odle, 1982).

One important finding from the SBA data base is that, even in periods of relative stability or modest growth in total employment, individual establishments are subject to wildly different but largely offsetting fluctuations. For example, the SBA estimates that from 1980 through 1986 private employment grew by 10.5 million jobs—an increase of 13 percent, or about 2 percent per year (see Table 3–1). However, this 13 percent growth was by no means uniform. New establishments and expanding

Table 3–1. Share of employment growth and its components due to small businesses, 1980–1986 (percentages)

	Proportionate change in employment due to component	Share of component due to small firms	
		Fewer than 100 employees	Fewer than 500 employees
Gross change due to:			
Births	39.5	40.2	53.9
Deaths	−31.3	41.8	56.3
Expansions	15.8	46.3	60.2
Contractions	−11.0	29.4	44.8
Net increase, 1980–1986	13.0	53.0	63.5
Initial (1980) employment	—	35.0	50.9

Source: Small Business Administration, 1988a, tables 14 and A–25.

establishments accounted for 44.5 million additional jobs (55 percent of initial employment), while 34 million jobs (42 percent of initial employment) were lost to contractions and closings of establishments. Thus, roughly 40 percent of the 80 million jobs represented in the SBA data base in 1980 had disappeared six years later; fortunately, this loss was offset by an even larger number of newly created jobs.

Has this micro chaos always existed within the framework of macro stability, or is it peculiar to the 1980s? Unfortunately, we know of no data that permit analogous calculations before the 1960s. But calculations by David Birch (1981) based on data from the 1970s similar to the SBA's, and analysis of Census of Manufacturers data since 1963 (Dunne, Roberts, and Samuelson, 1987) show a pattern quite similar to that described above.

The "job gains" and "job losses" described by these calculations are sums of changes in number of jobs in individual establishments. Although they suggest that many workers must have changed jobs, the fact that a job was "lost" to an establishment does not mean that the job was necessarily "lost" to any individual. For example, contracting businesses may reduce employment by not replacing those who quit or retire, without laying off any individual worker. There is some evidence that the majority of the (more modest) employment reductions that accompany increases in the minimum-wage are accomplished by not replacing quitters or by not making normal seasonal hires, rather than by discharges or layoffs (Converse et al., 1981, p. 282).

Small employers account disproportionately for the two most important components of employment change—the births and deaths of businesses. This phenomenon raises questions about the duration of the jobs created by small employers—a question we explore in greater detail below.

Small Business and Job Generation

If new jobs—to accommodate not only new entrants but also the larger number needed to offset establishments contracting and closing—are important to maintaining the overall pattern of relative stable growth revealed by aggregate statistics, then discovering where such job creation takes place is obviously of interest.

The SBA data bases have been used extensively in recent years to answer this question. While some attention has been given to geographic and industrial patterns of job creation, most of the emphasis—and, clearly, our emphasis as well—has focused on differences in job creation by firms of different sizes. The much-publicized conclusion is that small firms contribute a disproportionate share of new jobs.

Evidence in support of this conclusion is presented in Table 3–2. Since firms with fewer than 500 workers account for about 50 percent of the

Table 3–2. Share of small business in job growth, 1976–1986 (percentages)

Years	Firms with fewer than 100 employees	Firms with fewer than 500 employees
1976–1978	56.0	71.1
1978–1980	37.7	45.2
1980–1982	88.8	96.1
1982–1984	64.6	76.6
1984–1986	44.3	52.2
1976–1982	46.5	59.7
1980–1986	53.0	63.5

Sources: Small Business Administration, 1987, p. 63; 1988a, p. 38.

jobs in these data, in two of the five most recent two-year periods (1978–1980 and 1984–1986) small business accounted for about the same proportion of new jobs as its share of existing jobs. In the other three two-year periods, small business generated a clearly disproportionate share of new jobs. Focusing on firms with fewer than 100 workers, which employ about 35 percent of all workers, does not alter these conclusions.

When the calculation is repeated for six-year instead of two-year intervals, the small business's share of job creation is still greater than its share of current employment, but the difference is much smaller. One might expect small business's share of job growth over six years to equal the average of its share in the two-year subperiods. The reason this need not happen is that a firm that changes size may be in different categories in different two-year periods. For example, a firm that grew from "small" (fewer than 100 employees) to "large" (more than 100) in 1983 is treated as small in the 1980–1986 calculation and as small in 1980–1982 and 1982–1984, but as large in 1984–1986. A large firm that became small would be treated symmetrically.

The wide swings from one two-year period to another in the share of new jobs contributed by small firms reflects at least in part the major shocks that hit the economy in the past decade. The near-monopoly of small business on new jobs in 1980–1982 is probably the result of the severe recession, which took a heavy toll on employment in large manufacturing firms; the less impressive relative performance of small business in the years 1984–1986 may reflect the falling dollar's stimulation of exports by larger firms. It is too early to know whether proportionate or disproportionately large contributions by small business to job growth should be expected in the next decade. But in the decade covered by the table, small business's share of new jobs is clearly impressive.

Impressive, that is, compared with its share of employment. An alternative is to compare the growth of new jobs in small businesses with the growth of employment in *industries* dominated by small businesses. According to SBA tabulations (1986b), industries in which 60 percent or more of the workers are employed by small businesses account for about half of private-sector employment. From December 1981 (the first year for which data are available) to December 1986, these industries accounted for 85 percent of the increase in net employment (SBA, 1988b, p. 73). Thus, the growth of small business industries seems to be more impressive than the job generation of small businesses per se.

Do Small Firms Grow Faster?

Suppose we accept the message of Table 3–2 that small business has contributed a disproportionate share of new jobs and assume it will continue
to do so. One should *not* conclude from this that small firms grow faster
than large ones. In fact among firms that exist in one year, on average
their employment will be lower a few years later, and small firms will lead
this decline.

One cannot see these facts clearly in Table 3–1; the "births" referred
to there are births of establishments, whether new firms or part of existing ones. Fortunately, data from Birch (1987) for 1981–1985 allow us to
subtract jobs created by new establishments at existing firms from the
new-establishment total, in order to count jobs attributable to new firms.
In addition to the "standard" job-generation table, Birch presents sepa-
rate tabulations for single- and multiple-establishment firms. One com-
ponent of the single-establishment figures is the number of new jobs created by births of establishments in single-establishment firms—that is,
new single-establishment firms. Whereas the net increase in total
employment was 2.9 million jobs, the increase resulting from the creation
of single-establishment firms was 7.0 million. Consequently, existing
firms must have contracted by 4.1 million jobs, or about 6.4 percent of
their original level of employment.[1]

The finding that existing firms shrink on average does not apply only to
the period 1981–1985. Birch's data (1987, figs. 2.1 and 2.2) show that, on
average, employment in firms existing in 1969 had declined 27 percent by
1976. William Brock and David Evans (1986, tables 6.2 and 6.3) find a
similar decline for the years 1976–1982. Firms not busy being born are
busy dying—and this dying offsets the growth of those that survive.

Not only do existing firms on average shrink over time; the damage
tends to be more severe in small firms than in large ones. Most studies
do find that, *among surviving firms*, small firms grow more rapidly than
large ones.[2] But small businesses have very high mortality rates. (A
recent paper argued that *only* three out of five fail within their first five
years, whereas the conventional wisdom had said four out of five—see
Phillips and Kirchhoff, 1988). Although the mortality rate for established
small businesses is lower, it is still higher than for large firms. These mortality rates dominate the faster growth rates of small firms among the
survivors. Our analysis of Birch's data for 1981–1985 suggests that

employment in small firms (fewer than 500 workers) existing in 1981 declined by about 10 percent over the next four years, while employment in large firms existing in 1981 remained essentially unchanged. Data for 1969–1976 (Birch, 1987) and for 1976–1982 (Brock and Evans, 1986) also show that if calculations are extended to include all firms existing in the initial year, and not just those that survived, small businesses declined faster than large ones. Ariel Pakes and Richard Ericson (1989) report that 36.5 percent of Wisconsin firms active in 1978, but only 14.5 percent of those with more than 50 employees, had closed by 1986.

If small firms do not grow faster than large ones, how can they account for a disproportionate share of new employment? It is an accident of birth—new firms happen to be born small. Since new businesses account for more than 100 percent of the net increase in employment, and new businesses rarely start out with 100 or more employees, it is almost inevitable that small firms will account for a disproportionate share of new employment. Once established, however, small firms are not on average very hardy.

Changes in Small Business's Share of Total Employment

The image of small business as a disproportionate job generator might lead one to expect that the proportion of the workforce employed by small companies is growing rapidly. In fact, there is little evidence that this is the case.

Table 3–3 summarizes trends for the years 1958–1982, based on data from the censuses of business conducted every five years by the U.S. Census Bureau. The industrial coverage is incomplete: transportation, communications, public utilities, finance, insurance, and real estate and some service industries are excluded; and construction is included for the first time in 1967. Still, and despite the unavailability of results from the 1987 census, they provide the best evidence for any extended period. The message of Table 3–3 is straightforward: from 1958 to 1982 there was little change in the importance of small business. The small business share fluctuates by a few percentage points over each five-year period, but the small business share is no higher at the end of the period than it was at the start.

Since the results of the 1987 census of business are not yet available,

Table 3–3. Percentage of employment in small businesses, 1958–1982

Year	Firms with fewer than 100 employees		Firms with fewer than 500 employees	
	Excluding construction firms	Including construction firms	Excluding construction firms	Including construction firms
1958	41.3	—	55.1	—
1963	39.9	—	52.9	—
1967	37.4	39.9	50.2	53.2
1972	—	41.3	—	53.5
1977	—	40.1	—	52.5
1982	—	41.0	—	54.1

Sources: U.S. Census Bureau, U.S. Enterprise Statistics for 1958 through 1982, as reported in Small Business Administration, 1984 (table A2–24), 1987 (table 1–11).

Note: For sectors excluded in all years see text.

Table 3–4. Percentage of employment in small businesses, 1976–1986

Year	Firms with fewer than 100 employees	Firms with fewer than 500 employees
1976	36.3	50.4
1978	36.5	50.8
1980	35.0	49.5
1982	35.6	50.2
1984	36.2	50.9
1986	35.0	49.7

Source: Small Business Administration, unpublished tabulations, 1987.

the only way to update this conclusion is to switch to the SBA data base. The message of Table 3–4 is unmistakable: there is no trend here, either.

Small business's share of employment reflects both changes in its share in specific industries and changes in the importance of industries dominated by small firms. Table 3–5 shows trends within industries from 1958 to 1986. In the period 1958–1977 the small business share declined in each major industry group. More recently, it has rebounded slightly in mining, construction, and manufacturing but continued to drop in the much-publicized trade and service sectors. Thus, although employment has shifted

Table 3–5. Change in small firms' usage of employment, by industry, 1958–1986

	Firms with fewer than 500 employees	
Industry	1958–1977	1976–1986
Mining	−16.8	+7.8
Construction	−4.4[a]	+3.5
Manufacturing	−8.2	+1.8
Wholesale trade	−5.3	−0.8
Retail trade	−10.3	−7.5
Services	−8.4	−3.2

Sources: 1958–1977: U.S. Census Bureau, U.S. Enterprise Statistics for 1958 through 1977, as reported in Small Business Administration, 1984, table A2–24; 1976–1986: Small Business Administration, unpublished tabulations, 1987.

a. 1967–1977 only.

toward industries dominated by smaller firms, it has shifted *away* from small firms in those industries!

The stability of the small business share is difficult to understand if one's image of small firms is as prodigious job generators. It is not surprising if one recognizes that existing firms—and especially small ones—are on average shrinking, but that many new firms enter each year to offset that decline. Moreover, really successful small businesses grow until they become large—and no longer contribute to small business's share of employment.

Stability of Small Business Jobs

Given the high mortality rates of small companies, it will come as no surprise that the studies of firms' employment dynamics using the SBA data base show somewhat higher job-loss rates for small firms.

The job-loss rate generally employed in such studies is equal to jobs lost as a result of contractions or closings of establishments as a proportion of all employment. We can infer from the statistics in Table 3–1 that in the 1980–1986 period, small businesses accounted for 53.3 percent of these job losses, a proportion that slightly exceeds their 50.9 percent employment share.

Actually, Table 3–1 is likely to understate just how high the rate of job loss in small companies really is. The reason is that it takes a while for firms to find their way into the Dun and Bradstreet file—Phillips and Kirchhoff (1988) cite a figure of two years, but argue that this is an over-estimate. Thus, firms that survive only a short time are likely to be over-looked. Although the direction of this bias is clear, its magnitude is not. It may be that such firms vanish with so few workers that their inclusion would not appreciably change the results shown in Table 3–1.

An alternative to focusing on rates of job loss is to compare the expected duration of a job in different employment settings. Timothy Dunne and Mark Roberts (1987) do this for manufacturing workers; unfortunately for our purposes, they link expected duration to factors related to firm size (age of establishment, and single- or multiple-estab-lishment firm) rather than to firm size itself. They find that "younger plants have lower employment retention rates" (p. 22), as do establish-ments that are not part of a multiple-establishment firm.

Policy Implications

The record of small firms in generating jobs is sometimes seen as strengthening the case for a government policy that is sympathetic to small business. Suppose one rejects our reinterpretation of the evidence on job generation and ignores the fact that jobs with larger firms are likely to be more durable (Dunne, Roberts, and Samuelson, 1987) and to have higher wages and better working conditions, a point stressed in this con-text by Barry Bluestone and Bennett Harrison (1982). Does it follow that a policy favorable to small business is a logical implication of its job-gen-erating success?

In our view it does not. Of course it makes sense to consider relaxing a regulation that does little besides employ regulators. And doing so may well disproportionately assist small business. But the case for eliminating inefficient regulations need not rest on the virtues of small business.

Now consider a proposed change in the business environment: a tax change, repeal of a costly but effective environmental regulation, etc. Does the better job-generating record of small business argue that changes in business climate should be tilted to favor small firms?

The position of the policymaker is similar to that of a mythical Demo-cratic campaign chairman who served back in the days before the deceased of Chicago had been completely disfranchised. Noting that Cook County had always generated a disproportionate number of votes for the

Party, he considered concentrating his budget and other resources there. However, he quickly realized that he was likely to get a lot of votes there anyway, and spending *extra* dollars there might generate few *additional* votes. He realized, or seemed to realize, that allocation decisions depend—or ought to depend—on marginal effects rather than on average performance. Evidence that small firms generate more than their share of new jobs is as consistent with a claim that the playing field has steadily been tilted too far in their favor as it is with the view that further help is in order. There is no evidence that concentrating tax benefits or regulatory relief on small business rather than concentrating it elsewhere will generate more new jobs.

There may well be valid reasons for assisting small business—a subject that we discuss in Chapter 10. But even a favorable reading of the evidence on job generation does not in itself constitute a good case for doing so. Indeed, the extremely high mortality rate of small firms, rather than their strength in generating jobs, seems the more plausible starting point for building such a case.

· 4 ·

Wages: Bigger Means More

There is a rule of survival for small business. There are
things that you want to have [in paying workers] and
things you can afford. You had better go with what you
can afford.

—Bill Ryan, president of Ryan Transfer Corporation

Differences in the working lives of employees in our society are often
summarized by a single measure—differences in wages. The disparities
in compensation between men and women, whites and blacks, and union
and nonunion workers are well documented and well known. For those
who work in small companies or locations, however, another wage gap
exists that is as large, pervasive, and persistent as some of these other
more highly publicized pay differentials.

Workers in big companies or locations earn over 30 percent more in
wages than their counterparts in small firms or at small workplaces. In
1983 employees in companies with fewer than 500 workers earned an
average of $5.89 per hour, those in larger companies an average of $8.41
per hour. The existence of such a pay gap by itself is not necessarily note-
worthy. The implications of this wage differential depend on why it exists.
If jobs in larger firms or establishments require more skill or training, then
greater compensation simply reflects the higher pay necessary to attract
and retain more highly skilled workers. If working conditions in larger
enterprises are worse than those in smaller firms because of increased
regimentation or bureaucracy, then larger enterprises might pay higher
wages as a form of "combat pay" to compensate their workers for inferior
working conditions. Higher wages in larger firms or workplaces could also
be part of a union avoidance strategy, in which the employer offers better
pay to ward off union organizing attempts.

If these theories explained the difference in pay between large and
small firms or locations, the gap would be unremarkable. The evidence
shows, however, that these factors explain only part of the pay gap. The
unexplained difference—about 10 percent—represents the premium
enjoyed by those who work in large firms and locations.

The Size-Wage Difference

As we stated earlier, higher pay for workers in large firms and workplaces is not just a recent phenomenon. Wage information from the 1890 Census shows that men who worked in larger manufacturing firms then earned higher pay than their counterparts in smaller firms (Goldin, 1986). Evidence from wage surveys during the 1930s also indicates that those who worked for larger employers earned higher pay. More recent evidence reveals that in the 1980s workers in big firms or big establishments continued to earn higher pay. Table 4–1 shows that according to data collected by the Census Bureau for the Bureau of Labor Statistics in the May 1983 Current Population Survey, workers in companies with 500 or more employees earned 35 percent more than those in small companies, and employees in locations with 100 or more workers earned 37 percent more than those in smaller workplaces. The magnitude of the size-wage premium becomes even clearer when compared with other well-known pay differentials: it is nearly as large as the gap between wages for males and females (measured as 36 percent in 1983), larger than the pay advantages enjoyed by union members (29 percent), and much larger than the white–black wage differential (14 percent) (Bureau of Labor Statistics, 1983).

A plausible explanation for differences in pay or other characteristics between large and small firms is to say that these simply represent differences between manufacturing industries, the traditional home of big business, and service industries, the heart of small business activity. Yet our research shows that even within the same industry, workers in big firms take home larger paychecks than workers in small ones. As Table 4–2

Table 4–1. Wage premiums by employee characteristic, 1979 and 1983 (percentage differences)

Employee characteristic	1979	1983
In big companies (500 or more)	33	35
In big locations (100 or more)	31	37
Unionized	29	29
White	15	14
Male	43	36

Source: Bureau of Labor Statistics, May 1979 Current Population Survey and May 1983 Current Population Survey.
Note: 1979 sample size = 14, 259; 1983 sample size = 15,780.

Table 4–2. Size-wage premiums, by industry, 1983 (percentage differences)

Industry	Percentage by which wages are higher	Industry	Percentage by which wages are higher
Mining		Utility and sanitation	
Big companies	29	Big companies	21
Big locations	15	Big locations	20
Construction		Wholesale trade	
Big companies	37	Big companies	30
Big locations	36	Big locations	19
Durable manufacturing		Retail trade	
Big companies	37	Big companies	16
Big locations	29	Big locations	23
Nondurable manufacturing		Finance, insurance, and real estate	
Big companies	33	Big companies	20
Big locations	23	Big locations	26
Transportation		Services	
Big companies	42	Big companies	29
Big locations	31	Big locations	30
Communication			
Big companies	33		
Big locations	12		

Source: Bureau of Labor Statistics, May 1983 Current Population Survey.
Note: Big companies are those with 500 or more employees; big locations are those with 100 or more employees.
Note: Sample size = 15,434.

reveals, workers in both large and small companies and locations earned more than employees in smaller economic units regardless of their industry. The pay gap is largest in manufacturing industries. In 1983 an employee working for a very large company in a durable manufacturing industry (producing such goods as steel or machine parts) earned 37 percent more than a worker in the same industry employed by a small firm; the differential between large and small workplaces was 29 percent. The difference in pay, though less dramatic, is still clearly evident in trade and service industries. In the retail trade sector, workers in large firms earned 16 percent more than their counterparts in small firms, and workers in large locations earned 23 percent more than those in small workplaces.

Large employers also pay higher wages in both metropolitan and non-metropolitan areas (Brown and Medoff, 1989). Thus, the higher wages are not just a reflection of the tendency for larger employers to locate in metropolitan areas, where wages are higher, a possibility raised by Rees and Shultz (1970, p. 185). Moreover, this fact leads us to doubt that large employers pay higher wages because they are larger than smaller employers relative to their pool of potential applicants, and hence must pay higher wages to attract enough workers of a given quality, as suggested by Weiss and Landau (1984).

Another potential explanation for the size-wage premium is differences in unionization rates. The argument would run that since large firms are more likely to be unionized, greater pay in these firms simply represents union gains. Here again the results of the May 1983 Current Population Survey show that this cannot be the only story behind the pay differential between large and small employers. Nonunionized workers in large companies earned 36 percent more than their counterparts in small nonunionized firms. Among nonunion locations, employees in large workplaces earned 39 percent more than those working at small locations. Unionization does affect the magnitude of the size-wage effect. In the May 1983 Current Population Survey, workers in large union firms earned only 14 percent more than their counterparts in small union firms; workers in large union locations earned 9 percent more than those in small union locations. Unionization thus dampens the size-wage premium, perhaps because of the prevalence of union contracts which "take wages out of competition" by equalizing them across firms. Overall, however, explaining the size-wage premium involves more than simply attributing differences between large and small employers to the differences between manufacturing and services or to the differences between union and non-unionized operations.

The Role of Greater Skills

One reason large employers may pay higher wages is that they hire better workers. Large employers may find it more profitable to hire high-quality workers (and hence pay higher wages to compensate them) than do small employers. As we saw in Table 2–4, the workers in large firms do on average have more education and work experience than those in small firms. Yet this explanation for higher pay raises a further question: why would large employers find it more profitable to hire better workers than small firms do? One hypothesis is that larger locations make greater use of machinery in their production processes, which performs better when operated by higher-quality labor. As a result, these larger units find it profitable to hire more-skilled workers (Hamermesh, 1980).

In hiring workers, firms face the problem of finding employees who will perform their jobs without constant monitoring. As the size of a firm or location increases, monitoring each worker's productivity and performance is thought to become more difficult, and thus more expensive (Stigler, 1962). One solution is to spend more on screening job applicants, and studies confirm that larger employers do (Barron, Black, and Lowenstein, 1987). In addition, large employers may choose to hire better-quality workers in the beginning so that even though they cannot monitor on-the-job skill accumulation as effectively as small firms, they still end up with the needed pool of skills. Finally, the fact that larger employers spend more on securing the requisite labor is consistent with large firms' paying higher wages to reduce turnover, since the cost of screening and training must be borne whenever a replacement is hired.

While all these explanations link higher wages with higher worker quality, actual studies of differences in compensation between large and small firms and workplaces indicate that worker quality accounts for only part of the employer-size wage gap. It is true that workers in large firms tend to be older, more experienced, and more educated. As a result of these and other related regularities, part of the pay difference between large and small firms can be traced to the fact that large companies hire a more skilled workforce.

Yet the fact remains that, even after controlling for observable indicators of labor quality such as education and experience, nearly every study we know of finds that larger firms or locations pay higher wages (Masters, 1969; Stolzenberg, 1978; Mellow, 1982; Garen, 1985). The estimates presented in Table 4–3 support this finding. The data from the 1979 and 1983 May Current Population Surveys indicate that of two workers who are the same in terms of sex, race, education experience, industry, and occupation, the worker in the large firm will on average earn 10 to 13 percent more than the worker in the small firm. The data from the 1974 Employer Expenditures for Employee Compensation Survey show a slightly smaller advantage. Although this source takes into account fewer employee characteristics, the data are reported by firms rather than by workers, and thus provide an accurate indication of the cost of nonwage

Table 4–3. Size-wage premiums and labor quality (percentage differences)

Survey and compensation measure	Factors taken into account	Big-company wage advantage
May 1979 Current Population Survey (13,829 employees) Usual hourly wage	Union status, sex, race, age, education, Standard Metropolitan Statistical Area, region, detailed industry and occupation, tenure	10
May 1983 Current Population Survey (15,245 employees) Usual hourly wage	Same	13

1974 Employer Expenditures for Employee Compensation Survey (4,605 establishments)
  Hourly wage
  Total compensation
    per hour worked
	Union status, Standard Metropolitan Statistical Area, region, 2-digit SIC industry	7
		
		11

Sources: Bureau of Labor Statistics, 1974, 1979, 1983.

compensation. According to this survey, when wages and the cost of fringe benefits per hour are used as the measure of compensation, the advantage of working for a large firm increases from 7 to 11 percent. (As the next chapter will show, firm size has an even greater proportional effect on fringe benefits than on wages.)

The surveys summarized in Table 4–3 tried to account for differences in labor quality by holding constant the worker characteristics most obviously related to earnings. Another way to see if the size-wage gap persists when worker quality is taken into account is to look at wage differences within very narrowly defined occupations, where one would not expect much variation in labor quality. Charles Brown and James Medoff (1988) analyzed data from the Area Wage Surveys, covering workers in thirty-two cities for the period 1968–1982, and the Professional, Administrative, Technical, and Clerical Worker Surveys (PATCs) for 1965–1982, both of which provide data from the Bureau of Labor Statistics on wage patterns within narrowly defined occupations. Both surveys confirm that for workers in the same occupation, wages are higher in larger workplaces. In addition, both surveys show that the pay premium associated with working for a large employer increased in size from the late 1960s to the early 1980s. The PATC data also show, perhaps surprisingly, that for the white-collar workers it covers, the advantage of working for a larger firm is greater than average in the entry grades of most jobs, and smaller (indeed, in some occupations negligible) in the highest grades.

Although these surveys provide information about observable measures of labor quality such as experience and education or detailed occupation, the remaining unexplained differences in wages could be due to dimensions of work quality not captured in the measures we use. The information in Table 4–4 addresses this by summarizing changes in individual workers' wages taking into account the size of their employers before and after job changes. By so doing, we can check whether a particular worker's wages increase with a move to a larger employer or decrease with a move in the opposite direction. This technique effectively holds constant the unmeasured dimensions of worker quality that remain the same over the period examined. According to information from the Survey Research Center's Quality of Employment Surveys in Table 4–4, a worker leaving a job in a small location for one in a large location would earn approximately 10 percent more in pay.[1] Thus, differences in worker

Table 4–4. Wage premiums from working in or moving to a big (100 or more employees) location (percentage differences)

	Factors taken into account	Big-employer wage advantage
Working in big location		
1.	Union status, age, education, tenure	12
2.	Union status, age, education, tenure, Standard Metropolitan Statistical Area, region, detailed industry and occupation	13
Moving from small to big location		
3.	Same as 1 but differences used	10
4.	Same as 2 but differences used	8

Sources: Survey Research Center, 1973 and 1977 Quality of Employment Surveys.
Note: Sample size = 445 employees.

quality account for an important part of the differences in pay between large and small firms and workplaces, but they cannot provide a complete explanation for the employer-size wage differential.

The Role of Working Conditions

Another explanation for the employer-size wage gap is that large employers may have to pay higher wages in order to attract employees if workers find working conditions in large work environments to be less desirable than those in small firms or workplaces. Many images of big business associate the work environment in large workplaces with greater reliance on rules and less freedom in action and scheduling (Masters, 1969; Stafford, 1980), a more impersonal atmosphere (Lester, 1967), or greater commuting distances (Scherer, 1976). Small workplaces, on the other hand, are seen as havens of freedom and flexibility and as antidotes to bureaucracy. As an East Coast furnishing supplier put it in arguing that small firms can offer lower pay because they have more enjoyable environments: "You don't need to put together as fancy a package when you're offering people the opportunity to work in an entrepreneurial environment. Give them what they can't get at a larger company—responsibility and a chance to affect some of the decisions, mainly—and they're happy" (Wojahn, 1984c, p. 48).

Trying to quantify the relative attractiveness of work sites is even more difficult than identifying the factors that create a pleasant working environment. Not surprisingly, no survey provides a widely accepted index of the quality of working conditions. The data analyzed in Table 4–5, however, provide some evidence on the role of working conditions in explaining the employer-size wage gap. One way to account for differences in work environments is to take into account an employee's (narrowly defined) industry and occupation. The wage differential between big and small employers cannot be explained simply by differences in the relative attractiveness of working environments across industry and occupation, for the data in Table 4–5 show that even within the same detailed occupation and industry there is a large wage differential between big and small employers.

Table 4–5 also incorporates evidence on working conditions from the Quality of Employment Surveys (last conducted by the Survey Research Center at the University of Michigan in 1977), which provide data about

Table 4–5. Size-wage premiums by working conditions (percentage differences)

Survey	Factors taken into account	Employer unit	Big-employer wage advantage
1. May 1979 Current Population Survey (13,829 employees)			
a.	Union status, sex, race, education, work experience, Standard Metropolitan Statistical Area, region	Company	12
b.	Same as 1a plus 2-digit census industry, major census occupation	Company	10
c.	Same as 1a plus 3-digit census industry, detailed census occupation	Company	10
2. 1973 and 1977 Quality of Employment Survey (445 employees)			
a.	Same as 1a plus year	Location	12
b.	Same as 2a plus 2-digit census industry, major census occupation	Location	13
c.	Same as 2b plus direct assessments of working conditions	Location	12
3. 1973 and 1977 Quality of Employment Survey (445 employees) (analysis based on 1973-to-1977 differences)			
a.	Equivalent to 2a but differences used	Location	10
b.	Equivalent to 2b but differences used	Location	7
c.	Equivalent to 2c but differences used	Location	6

Sources: Bureau of Labor Statistics, 1979; Survey Research Center, 1973 and 1977.

an employee's workplace size, job conditions, wages, and other key factors. The job conditions focused on in the surveys under discussion include those most likely to vary by employer size: weekly hours, working on the second or third shift, choice about overtime work, dangerous or unhealthy conditions, unpleasant work conditions, and commuting time. The results indicate that this direct information on working conditions explains very little of the size-wage effect. Including other factors intended to measure more elusive working conditions such as pace of work (Oi and Raisian, 1985), relationships with coworkers and supervisors, and perceived job security adds little to the explanations of the size-wage premium (Brown and Medoff, 1989). The effect of taking all these working conditions into account was a slight increase in the premium associated with working at a large location—the exact opposite of what one would expect if larger workplaces had inferior working conditions.[2]

As a final blow to the theory that larger firms and workplaces pay higher wages because of less favorable working conditions, the Quality of Employment Survey responses provide no direct evidence that working conditions are less desirable in larger locations. Of the 42 job characteristics considered, only 21 grew less desirable as location size increased, and nearly all of these differences were small enough to result from chance. Although this evidence does not rule out the possibility that working conditions account for some of the large size-wage premium, the results indicate that such conditions are very unlikely to have much explanatory power.

The Role of Union Avoidance

Large employers are frequently said to pay higher wages in order to avoid unionization. Studies of nonunion firms provide qualitative evidence that these companies often try to pay the same wages as unionized businesses. Fred Foulkes (1982) also found that the practices of their unionized competitors were very much on the minds of executives in nonunion firms. In the words of the executives interviewed by Foulkes,

> The company pays a slight premium in its nonunion plants over the wages paid in the general geographic area for similar work at union plants.

> Because we are such a union target, we find that we have to get our start rate at or about at the union rate.

Cost-of-living clauses are not uncommon in our industry, though the uncapped nature of ours does distinguish us. But you also have to remember that, in our area, the United Auto Workers, which have cost-of-living, are strong.

Our people are treated well. We have what the unions want. That is our goal.   (Foulkes, pp. 47, 151, 154, 165)

Similarly, experts in keeping workplaces nonunion typically advise their large clients to "try to do what the union does for its employees, but to do it better" (Freeman and Medoff, 1984, p. 15). Large nonunion employers may feel more threatened by unions, who view them as potential "cash cows." They may therefore do more for their employees in order to avoid losing their nonunion status.

Despite the plausibility of this explanation, union avoidance strategies do not appear to play a key role in causing large firms to pay higher wages. Table 4–6 presents evidence from the 1979 and 1983 Current Population Surveys that supports this claim. The first line of the table shows the extra pay associated with working for a large company among nonunion workers in general (taking into account such factors as education, experience, and

Table 4–6. Size-wage premiums in big (500 or more employees) nonunion firms, by employee group, 1979 and 1983 (percentage differences)

Nonunion employee group[a]	Wage advantage	
	1979	1983
All private nonfarm wage-and-salary workers	9	13
Managers and administrators	10	11
Professional, technical, and related workers	9	13
Workers in 3-digit census occupations with union membership percentage ≤ 5%	8	10
Workers in 3-digit census industries with union membership percentage ≤ 5%	9	9

Sources: Bureau of Labor Statistics, May 1979 and May 1983 Current Population Surveys.
   a. Factors taken into account: union status, sex, race, age, education, tenure, Standard Metropolitan Statistical Area, region, detailed industry and occupation.

industry); this should be seen as a benchmark. The next four lines present the same statistic for four groups of workers for whom the likelihood of unionization is minimal. If union avoidance efforts were an important part of the size-wage relationship, the effect would be much weaker for workers who seem unlikely to seek unions. However, it is not. In addition, even among unionized employees, those in large firms and large locations are paid more—despite unions' general desire to "take wages out of competition" by negotiating contracts that call for similar wages at different firms. As a result, we feel confident in concluding that the size-wage premium is not a result of attempts by large employers to remain union free.

The Role of Monitoring

Another potential explanation for the size-wage premium is based on the belief that monitoring employees to prevent them from shirking on the job is much more difficult in large firms. As a result, large employers pay more than the market dictates so that their employees will fear being discharged if they are caught shirking. Under this hypothesis, the size-wage premium is a policing device.[3]

Kruse (1989) finds that those who are more closely supervised receive wages that are slightly lower than those of other workers. But the smallness of this effect and the apparently weak relationship between reported supervision and establishment size means that controlling for workers' reports of the intensity of supervision on the job does not change the estimated size-wage premium.

A decisive piece of evidence against the monitoring hypothesis comes from an analysis of wage differentials among workers paid by the piece. Here, monitoring should be much less of an issue or none at all. Our analysis of data in the Bureau of Labor Statistics Industry Wage Surveys indicates that piece-rate workers for large employers receive higher wages than those working for small ones; in fact the size-wage premium is, if anything, larger for piece-rate workers than for employees paid an hourly wage.[4]

The Role of Discounts

The questions of how, in a reasonably competitive economy, large employers can afford to pay higher wages and why they do so are very different. Many believe that large employers have monopoly power in their product markets, which allows them to charge above competitive prices. Empirical work on this matter does not support the contention that (for whatever reason) large employers are sharing their monopoly profits with their workers.[5]

An alternative factor that might explain how large employers can pay their workers more is that they pay a lot less for their nonlabor inputs (which represent a very sizable fraction of their total expenditures). Table 4–7 sheds light on the extent of discounts through a statistical analysis of data from the 1982 Census of Manufacturers.[6] It shows that quantity discounts on key nonlabor inputs are pervasive and deep. Similarly, larger loans (which are typically made to larger borrowers) carry considerably lower interest rates (see Table 4–8).

A preliminary analysis with data from the Bureau of Labor Statistics 1979 Wage Distribution Survey indicates that much of the wage premium offered by large employers could be financed by the price discounts received on large purchases of nonlabor inputs. After taking into account

Table 4–7. Quantity discounts on fuel prices for large purchasers,[a] 1982 (percentage differences)

Fuel	Cross-industry analysis (4-digit SIC manufacturing industries)[b]	Cross-state analysis (2-digit SIC manufacturing cells)[c]
Coal	19	9[d]
Distilled oil	7	4
Electricity	26	25
Liquified petroleum gases	6[d]	9
Natural gas	6	13
Residual oil	3[d]	−1[d]

Source: U.S. Census Bureau, data tape for 1982 Census of Manufacturers (Washington, D.C.).

a. Large purchasers are establishments that purchase quantities one standard deviation above average. Analyses compare these with establishments purchasing quantities one standard deviation below average.

b. Sample sizes range from 40 industries for coal to 434 for electricity.

c. Sample sizes range from 59 cells for coal to 715 for electricity.

d. Results not statistically significant at conventional levels.

Table 4–8. Rates charged by all banks on loans, May 6–10, 1985 (percent)

Loan size (thousands of dollars)	Short-term loans		Long-term loans	
	Fixed rate	Floating rate	Fixed rate	Floating rate
1–24	14.1	13.1		
25–49	13.4	12.7	16.0	13.1
50–99	13.3	12.7		
100–499	12.8	12.2	12.8	12.2
500–999	10.4	11.5	11.8	11.5
1,000+	9.1	10.5	10.0	10.4

Source: Board of Governors, Federal Reserve System, "Survey of Terms of Banks Lending," Statistical Release E.2 (Washington, D.C., 1985), in Small Business Administration, 1986, p. 51.

workers' age and sex, their union status, and their industry of employment, we find that the magnitude of the large-employer wage premium is much more substantial where the fraction of total costs incurred in securing inputs other than labor is big than where it is not. The size of the large-employer wage premium appears to be closely related to the pool of discounts on nonlabor inputs available to large employers. However, an analysis of Current Population Survey data did not replicate this result. Consequently, it is not clear whether the discounts shown in Tables 4–7 and 4–8 explain how large employers might be able to pay their workers more than the market dictates and still survive.

Again, why they do so is another question. At this time, the answer to this is still an open research question. Even when such factors as worker quality, working conditions, and the threat of unionization are taken into account, a size-wage premium remains to be enjoyed by workers in large firms and large locations.

· · ·

Both larger firms and larger locations pay substantially higher wages to their employees—about one-third more than small companies and workplaces. Even when differences in worker quality are taken into account, the size-wage premium remains at 10 to 15 percent. This wage gap cannot be explained by differences in working conditions or by union avoidance strategies. Although the complete explanation for the size-wage premium remains elusive, the bottom line for employees is clear: on average, going to work for a large employer pays, and pays very well.

Who Benefits?

Even though small businesses are providing jobs for
growing segments of the labor force, most small businesses are likely to offer fewer and less comprehensive
fringe benefits than larger businesses. The gap between
small and large firm coverage has not narrowed . . .

— Small Business Administration, 1985

More than 30 million Americans live without any health insurance today,
uncertain about how they will pay their medical bills and threatened by
financial ruin in case of illness. This is the situation not only of the poor—
minorities, the infirm, and the jobless—but also of 8.2 million private
wage-and-salary workers. Of these people who have a job but no health
insurance, 6.1 million work in firms with fewer than 500 employees. Also
lacking coverage are 1.6 million business owners, most of them owners
of small firms (SBA, 1987). Thus, for many Americans, employment in a
small business and lack of health insurance go hand in hand.

The distribution of health care benefits reflects a general pattern of
employee benefit coverage. Large firms not only pay their employees
higher wages; they also provide markedly better fringe benefits than
those of smaller firms. Many of the reasons offered for the employer-size
wage gap also help explain why large firms offer higher compensation in
terms of fringe benefits. The different costs of providing these benefit
programs in small and large firms may also contribute to the disparity in
the quantity and quality of fringes offered. What to do about differentials
in privately funded benefits is controversial, as the current debate over
mandating employer provision of health care, parental leave, and other
fringes demonstrates. What is not controversial, however, is the fact that
the benefits of workers who work for large employers are significantly
better than the benefits of those who work for employers that are small.

Small businesses often fail to offer fringe benefits almost universally
available from large firms. Table 5–1 shows that in a 1986 study conducted
for the Small Business Administration, every firm sampled with more than
500 employees offered a health insurance plan, compared with 55 percent

Table 5–1. Percentage of large and small businesses offering various fringe benefits, 1986

Fringe benefit	Firms with 500 or more employees	Firms with fewer than 500 employees
Vacation	95	58
Health	100	55
Sick leave	91	36
Life insurance	94	29
Pension or 401K	79	16
Bonus plan	29	11
Short-term disability	55	10
Long-term disability	69	9
Savings plan	29	2
Cafeteria-style health benefits	12	1
Vacation, sick, health, life, and pension or 401K	75	7

Source: Adapted from ICF, 1987.

of firms with fewer than 500 workers. The disparity for sick leave and life insurance was even greater: 94 percent of large firms had life insurance programs for employees, compared with 29 percent of small businesses; and 91 percent of large employers offered sick leave programs, in contrast to 36 percent of small employers. The large businesses had an overall edge in fringes: 75 percent offered their employees paid vacation, sick leave, health and life insurance, and some form of pension/retirement plan; only 7 percent of the small businesses provided this package.[1]

Because we expect the largest of the "small" firms to provide better benefits than the smallest of the "small," counting the proportion of firms that provide certain benefits may understate the proportion of workers who receive such benefits. Table 5–2 deals with this issue, for it presents information from the Current Population Survey for May 1979 and May 1983 on the percentage of *workers* in each size category who have particular benefits. Nonunion blue collar employees and white collar workers are much more likely to work for a firm with a retirement plan and health insurance if they work for a large firm (500 or more workers) rather than a small firm. This pattern also holds among unionized blue-collar workers.

Additional evidence on the coverage of workers comes from the Survey Research Center's Quality of Employment Survey (1977), which exam-

Table 5–2. Percentage of employees in big and small businesses with retirement and health plans, 1979 and 1983

	Blue-collar nonunion		Blue-collar union		White-collar	
	Firms with 500 or more employees	Firms with fewer than 500 employees	Firms with 500 or more employees	Firms with fewer than 500 employees	Firms with 500 or more employees	Firms with fewer than 500 employees
Retirement plan						
1979	60	13	87	75	74	31
1983	62	13	88	69	71	30
Health insurance plan						
1979	77	36	96	85	86	58
1983	76	37	96	85	86	60

Sources: Bureau of Labor Statistics, May 1979 and May 1983 Current Population Surveys.

Table 5–3. Percentage of nonunion employees in different-sized locations with various fringe benefits, 1977

Fringe benefit	Number of employees in location			
	1–49	50–99	100–499	500+
Retirement plan	41	53	72	90
Medical insurance	60	73	85	95
Dental benefits	14	15	29	43
Eyeglass benefits	6	10	19	29
Life insurance	44	60	72	87
Paid vacation	74	84	90	96
Thrift plan	21	38	46	63
Maternity leave with pay	14	39	33	47
Maternity leave with full reemployment rights	54	72	77	90
Day care	1	2	3	3
Sick leave	56	65	67	83
Profit sharing	23	27	32	31
Stock options	13	11	27	43
Free or discounted meals	18	24	13	22
Free or discounted merchandise	33	39	30	50
Legal aid	7	7	9	14

Source: Survey Research Center, 1977 Quality of Employment Survey, in Medoff, 1987.

ines workers' benefit coverage and the size of the workplace. Tables 5–3 and 5–4 imply that the disparity in fringe benefits evident between large and small firms also holds for large and small establishments. Among non-union workers in establishments with 100 or more employees, between 85 and 95 percent received medical insurance, and between 72 and 87 percent received life insurance. Among nonunion employees at locations with fewer than 100 workers, however, the comparable percentage ranges were only between 60 and 73 (for medical insurance) and between 44 and 60 (for life insurance). The story is the same for most other benefits. For instance, maternity leave with full reemployment rights, which was offered by the employers of more than 77 percent of the workers in nonunion establishments of 100 or more, was much less widespread among nonunion workers in smaller locations.

A comparison of Table 5–3 with Table 5–4 indicates that unionization tends to eliminate the difference between fringe benefit provision in small and large establishments. The percentages of workers employed in unionized locations with retirement plans, medical insurance, and life insurance are very similar regardless of workplace size.

All fringe benefit programs are not created equal. In fact programs can vary as much as the size of firms. Although both a large firm and a small one may offer a health care insurance program for employees, the larger firm's benefits are likely to be higher. The ICF study conducted in 1986 for the Small Business Administration found that nearly all company health programs covered hospital room and board, surgical care, lab procedures, and physician hospital care, but that larger firms were "more likely to cover office visits, home health care, maternity care, mental health, and other benefits" (ICF, 1987, p. ES4).

We noted in Chapter 4 that compensation per hour worked (which includes fringe benefits) differed even more with employer size than do hourly wages. Indeed, the EEEC data in Table 4–3 suggest that fringes per hour are more than 30 percent higher in large firms than in small ones.

The ultimate judges of the value of employee benefits are the employees. Table 5–5, based on data from a 1984 Harris survey for the AFL-CIO, shows that worker satisfaction with benefits grows with firm size. In firms with fewer than 500 employees, both blue-collar and white-collar workers were less satisfied with both fringes and pay than those working for larger firms. Forty-one percent of blue-collar nonunion workers in large firms said they were satisfied with their fringes, versus only 21 percent in small firms. The gap in satisfaction is less pronounced for unionized

Table 5–4. Percentage of union employees in different-sized locations with various fringe benefits, 1977

Fringe benefit	Number of employees in location			
	1–49	50–99	100–499	500+
Retirement plan	90	93	85	95
Medical insurance	88	98	98	96
Dental benefits	52	44	51	68
Eyeglass benefits	40	44	40	65
Life insurance	71	74	74	87
Paid vacation	59	71	89	92
Thrift plan	39	50	58	59
Maternity leave with pay	19	50	29	40
Maternity leave with full reemployment rights	94	89	94	85
Day care	2	0	0	2
Sick leave	64	62	51	49
Profit sharing	10	16	10	16
Stock options	9	12	15	29
Free or discounted meals	14	9	8	7
Free or discounted merchandise	21	26	30	41
Legal aid	7	13	10	4

Source: Survey Research Center, 1977. Quality of Employment Survey, in Medoff, 1987.

Table 5–5. Employees' satisfaction with fringe benefits and pay, 1984 (percentages)

	Firm size		Location size	
	500 or more employees	Fewer than 500 employees	100 or more employees	Fewer than 100 employees
Very satisfied with fringes				
Blue-collar nonunion	41	21	42	23
Blue-collar union	46	38	38	45
White-collar	52	36	53	37
Very satisfied with pay				
Blue-collar nonunion	25	23	22	24
Blue-collar union	47	33	43	43
White-collar	37	32	38	31

Source: Harris survey for the AFL-CIO, 1984.

workers, reflecting the smaller gap between fringes available in small and large firms that are unionized. The difference in worker satisfaction in large and small firms is much greater for fringe benefits than for wages, a result consistent with the fact that the employer-size gap is even greater for fringes than for wages.

Many of the explanations offered in Chapter 4 for why large employers offer higher wages also apply to fringes. Since wages and fringes together form employee compensation, larger firms may offer better fringes (like higher wages) in an attempt to secure and retain needed labor or to forestall unionization.

In addition, it may cost large firms less than it costs small firms to provide fringe benefits, because the overhead and administration costs of setting up and running a benefit program may not vary much with the number of workers covered; thus, the cost per worker of offering many benefits would be much lower in larger firms. The evidence on firm costs strongly bears this out. According to a 1984 report prepared for the Small Business Administration, a small business paid on average $1,080 per employee to establish a given pension plan, while it cost a large firm only $574 per worker to provide the same benefit (SBA, 1985). Emily Andrews (1989) reaches similar conclusions in a review of five studies. Her analysis of NFIB survey data shows that for small employers a 10 percent increase in the number of workers covered increases administrative costs by only 4 percent; as a result costs per worker fall by 6 percent.

An analogous pattern of higher costs for smaller firms prevails in health care insurance (ICF, 1987). The average monthly premium paid for company health care plans was about 10 percent higher for small businesses than for large ones. Firms with fewer than 500 workers paid on average $205 per employee per month in premiums for family coverage, whereas larger firms paid only $186. The nature of small business jobs and the type of workers hired by small business both help explain why fringe benefits such as health benefits cost small firms more. Extending the administrative cost argument, one study of the gap in health care benefits concluded that "smaller firms, which generally have higher employee turnover rates and seasonal employment, face higher administrative costs when trying to provide coverage for such workers" (ICF, 1987, p. 3-1).

In addition to the cost of monthly premiums for health care, there is the cost of setting up a health care plan—deciding how generous benefits should be, what the worker's contribution should be, and shopping among various providers. For large firms, this hard-to-quantify cost is spread over many employees. For small firms the cost per worker may be considerable; in fact it may explain small employers' reluctance, noted in the business press, to establish fringe benefit programs for their workers (Wojahn, 1984b, p. 106, and 1984c, pp. 49–50).

Finally, both analysts and businesspeople frequently cite lack of profitability of the business as a reason for the low level of fringe benefits in small firms. One line of argument is that small employers just cannot afford them; another is that small firms are less likely to have a sufficient profit margin to be able to deduct the cost of the fringes (SBA, 1985, p. 250; *Inc.*, September 1984). In our view, these cannot stand independently as explanations, since both poverty and tax considerations apply to wages as well as to fringes, and the ratio of fringes to wages is so much lower in small firms.

· · ·

Taken together, the results in Chapters 4 and 5 show that workers in small firms receive less in terms of both salary and fringes than their counterparts in large ones. Yet compensation is not the only measure of a job's desirability. The next chapter examines the other factors affecting workers' assessments of their experience with large and small employers.

· 6 ·

The Total Package

Growing awareness of small business' expanding role in
the economy has led to major changes in the way the
world looks at these businesses. Once thought of as
grubby, they are now often seen as glamorous, the
entrepreneur as folk hero.

—Richard Greene, *Forbes*, 1986

Surveying the opportunities for college graduates in the fall of 1987, the
editor of the *Wall Street Journal*'s career guide concluded: "Contrary to
public sentiment, small companies offer better career opportunities than
big business" (Pappas, 1987, p. 5). As the preceding chapters show,
workers in small firms receive lower wages and fewer fringe benefits than
comparable workers in large companies. Chapter 9 will show that workers
in smaller firms also have less regulatory protection. Yet the notion persists that there may be differences in job security or training, or intangible
differences in working environments, such as greater freedom and the
ability to get ahead in the company, that make it more worthwhile to work
for a small firm.

The arguments that job security and training opportunities are superior
in small firms are mistaken. Comparing the more personal aspects of the
work environment in big and small firms, such as opportunities for challenge and creativity, is harder. By definition, the intangibles that small
firms may offer cannot be measured. But indirect evidence fails to confirm
that there are unmeasured benefits from working in a small business that
leave workers as happy as they might be in large businesses. Whether
one looks at quit rates as a sign of job dissatisfaction or the number of
applicants per vacancy as an indicator of desirable jobs, the total package
of wages, benefits, and working conditions appears to be better in large
firms.

Job Security

A key question in the debate over whether large or small employers offer a better work environment is: how long will this work last? In an economy marked by both business downturns that lead to layoffs and business failures that lead to abrupt terminations, job security is an important element of the employment package. Stories about working in a small business often emphasize the failure rate of new businesses, which makes employment there quite unstable. But more common in the current career lore are stories about jobs lost in big business as a result of restructuring in the economy and the purported decline of American manufacturing. Thus, a 1986 article assessing employment prospects in large and small companies noted that

> big business has lost one of its major attractions for employees: job security. Over the last year Exxon, Du Pont, Black and Decker, Chevron, and AT&T have joined the ranks of other huge corporations that have laid off or squeezed out hundreds of thousands of employees, many middle management. Of course, it's true that a tiny company is far more likely to go out of business altogether than a big firm. But since there are no shareholders to quibble over a drop in quarterly earnings, a small firm is less likely to make layoffs just to keep earnings on track. (Greene, 1986, p. 156)

The reports of the death of job security in big firms are greatly exaggerated. The evidence suggests that employees in large establishments are actually less likely to be laid off than their counterparts in small workplaces.

News coverage of layoffs and terminations focuses on large workplaces rather than on small ones primarily because businesses are on average larger in the manufacturing sector, and this is where a very large proportion of layoffs occurs. Moreover, layoffs in a plant employing 500 people are often more visible than those in a struggling small business. Yet one study of U.S. manufacturing covering the period 1950–1971 found that a much smaller percentage of the workforce in large establishments was likely to be laid off each month than in small establishments (Medoff, 1979).

Data for 1980 and 1981 for California, Delaware, and Texas indicate that although large employers are more likely to be in high-layoff industries, within an industry jobs are more secure with large employers (Bowes, Brechling, and Jacobson, 1985). Overall layoff rates were lower for firms of 100 or more employees in California, for smaller firms in Delaware, and independent of firm size in Texas. In individual industries, however, layoffs were lower in large firms in California (41 of 43 industries) and Texas (26 of 43), and about the same (17 of 29) in Delaware. The negative relationship between employer size and layoffs within industries is slightly stronger if only employers of 500 or more are counted as large. In the one state (Delaware) in which temporary and permanent layoffs could be distinguished, permanent layoff rates were about three times as high in small firms as in large ones. Finally, a study of male workers for the years 1976–1981 found that larger employers "offer jobs that last longer, lead to fewer future job changes, and are less likely to lead to subsequent spells of unemployment" (Evans and Leighton, 1987, p. 7).

Training

The high percentage of young employees in small firms suggests that small firms offer many people a starting point for their careers (see Table 2–3). Bradley Schiller, who found that over two-thirds of American males got their first private-sector job in firms employing fewer than 500 workers, concluded: "The preponderant role of small businesses in providing initial work experience and training opportunities for the U.S. labor force is evident. It is also evident that many of the benefits of this early work experience are being reaped by larger firms" (Schiller, 1983, p. 85).

But the fact that many workers start out in small firms and later move to larger ones does not mean that they necessarily acquire their training in small businesses. Although work experience provides an opportunity to learn on the job, the question remains how the actual training received in small and large firms differs. John Bishop, who examined this very question in his work on occupational training (1982), found that new employees received far more hours of both formal and informal training in establishments with more than 500 workers than in smaller workplaces (see Table 6–1). One would expect more formal training in larger firms, because they can train more people in one "class" with a single instructor; but the more extensive informal training by coworkers at large firms is surprising. Bishop also concluded that training in larger establishments is more effective, because it brings about greater increases in productivity.

Other analyses have produced more mixed results. In a later study controlling for industry and occupation, Bishop (1985) found a curvilinear rela-

Table 6–1. Employee training during first 3 months in different-sized locations (hours)

	Number of employees at location				
	1–9	10–49	50–99	100–499	500+
Type of training					
Watching	49	44	54	49	60
Formal training	11	10	12	9	26
Informal training by management	59	44	51	46	57
Informal training by coworkers	22	24	25	28	52
Training time index	162	136	160	141	228

Source: Bishop, 1982, p. 11.

Note: As calculated by Bishop, the training time index is a weighted sum of hours spent in different categories of training, with the weights intended to reflect the cost to firms.

tionship between size and training, with smallest and largest establishments providing the most training. Analyzing the same (Employment Opportunity Pilot Project) data as Bishop, John Barron, Dan Black, and Mark Lowenstein (1987) found that the probability of formal and informal training rose with establishment size, but they did not find a statistically significant (linear) relationship between employer size and hours or weeks of training. Sheldon Haber's (1988) analysis of Bureau of Labor Statistics Survey of Income and Program Participation data showed that employees in large firms (at least 100 workers) were about twice as likely as those in small firms to have participated in a formal training program in their current workplace. Elizabeth Hill (1987) found no significant relationship between establishment size and the amount spent on training medium-skill technical workers, but she did (Hill, 1988) find larger establishments more likely to provide training that is useful at that firm, and no less likely to provide more general training. On balance, it appears that large employers provide more training. But the evidence is not overwhelming, perhaps because the most training is provided by both the very smallest and the largest firms.[1]

Intangibles

Once differences in wages, benefits, and the work environment are measured, there remain the "intangible" elements of a job, elements that proponents of small business say decidedly favor life in a small firm. As one *Forbes* article put it:

> few employees join a small company for job security. The pay isn't the lure for most people, either . . . So why does working for a smallish company turn people . . . on? Because of things that working for a big company can rarely offer: the proximity and guidance of an owner-founder, the potential for fast movement if the firm grows quickly, opportunities for a substantial equity interest somewhere down the line, and the ability to get involved in every-thing the company does. (Greene, 1986, p. 156)

One way to gauge employee satisfaction is to measure their tenure at a firm. Table 6–2 shows that, regardless of union or occupational status, workers in large firms stay with the same employer much longer than those in small firms. Part of this difference, however, may reflect the higher failure rate of small firms; hence the shorter job attachments there could stem in part from these firms' shorter lives. In addition, as we have just seen, larger firms make less use of layoffs than do comparable smaller firms.

A more refined measure of satisfaction with intangibles in the work environment is the quit rate of employees. Because larger firms and establishments offer higher wages and fringe benefits, lower quits there could reflect attachment to this higher compensation rather than satisfaction with noncompensation aspects of the job. Table 6–3 tries to take these factors into account by comparing quit rates among workers with the same wages. The results show that workers in large establishments historically have had much lower quit rates than their counterparts in small ones—the opposite of what one would expect if those in small locations enjoyed greater intangible benefits, and certainly not what one would

Table 6–2. Average years with different-sized employers, by employee group, 1983

Employee group	Number of employees in company				Number of employees at location			
	1–24	25–99	100–499	500+	1–24	25–99	100–499	500+
Blue-collar nonunion	4	4	5	7	4	4	6	9
Blue-collar union	6	8	9	12	8	9	10	13
White-collar	5	5	6	8	5	6	7	9

Source: Bureau of Labor Statistics, May 1983 Current Population Survey.

Table 6–3. Quit frequencies by establishment size

	Small establishments	Large establishments
Monthly quit rate (quits per 100 employees)		
State-by-2-digit SIC manufacturing cells, 1965–1969[a]	3.5	1.9
3-digit SIC manufacturing industries, 1958–1971[a]	2.1	1.7
Percent of employees changing jobs by quitting (1973–1977)		
Quality of Employment Survey, all industries (period rates)[b]	30	21

Note: The models on which these predicted rates were based took wage rates and other factors into account; see Medoff, 1979.

a. Large establishments are defined as those whose size is one standard deviation above the mean; small establishments are defined as those whose size is one standard deviation below the mean.

b. Large establishments are those defined as with 100 or more employees, small establishments as those with fewer than 100 employees.

expect if small locations had enough such intangibles to offset the lower wages they offer.[2]

Those who work for large employers may remain on their jobs longer not only because of more attractive wage and nonwage remuneration but also because of more opportunities to move from one assignment to another within the firm. There does appear to be more internal job movement among workers of large employers (Brown and Medoff, 1989). However, we found that even for workers who did not change detailed (three-digit census) occupations—for whom internal job movement should not be much of an issue—those working for large employers were less likely to change their employer. The fact that this was true even after wage differentials were taken into account strongly suggests that the ability to change jobs without leaving large employers does not explain the greater attachment to these employers.

If jobs in large firms are superior, those employers should have longer queues of qualified job applicants. The limited evidence available indicates that this is the case. The Survey Research Center in 1980 asked employers of minimum-wage workers: "If you were to have an opening for a minimum-wage job now, how many qualified applicants would you get?" The survey revealed that, whether worker characteristics were taken into account or not, larger employers reported significantly more appli-

applicat lists!

cants for the hypothetical vacancy. John Barron and John Bishop (1985) and Harry Holzer, Lawrence Katz, and Alan Krueger (1988) report similar findings in a broader sample of workers, using actual applications. Indeed, Holzer, Katz, and Krueger conclude that, with the wage rate held constant, "the size of an employer has a tremendous effect on the application rate. The number of applications per job opening rises sharply with establishment and firms size, all else [being held] equal" (p. 26).

The number of applicants per vacancy may reflect an employer's visibility in the local labor market as well as the desirability of jobs per se. The applicant findings are therefore consistent with the claim that larger employers offer better jobs, although by themselves these findings could perhaps be explained in other ways.

·   ·   ·

Although defining and assessing "opportunities" is difficult, the two-thirds of the survey respondents in a 1987 University of Michigan poll who said that big business is the "prime source of economic opportunity" are correct in terms of the wages, benefits, and working conditions offered by these firms. Small firms may be unable or unwilling to match the total package offered by their large counterparts. As the president of a 26-employee insurance agency explained the lack of a structured compensation system in his firm: "It's not that we're not goal-oriented; we just don't see the need to be so sophisticated, with bar graphs and bell curves. Any business under 50 employees is really run like a family. It has to be" (Wojahn, 1984c). For most workers in small businesses, however, their firms are families with thoroughly modern divorce rates.

· 7 ·

Employer Size and Unions

Small units should not be overlooked as organizing targets.
— AFL-CIO Committee on the Evolution of Work

Only 18 percent of the U.S. workforce is unionized. Large employers are much more likely than small ones to have unionized nonoffice workers. Table 7–1 documents this claim using data on unionization and size reported by employers. The table indicates that the percentage of establishments whose nonoffice workers are unionized rises steadily from 8 percent at sites with fewer than 50 nonoffice workers to 66 percent at sites with 1,000 or more. Although these data are more than a decade old (the Bureau of Labor Statistics survey from which they are drawn was discontinued in 1982), more recent worker-reported data show the same pattern (Table 7–2). Whether employer size is measured by employment at the workplace or in the company as a whole, those working for large employers are more likely to be unionized.

Table 7–1. Percentage of establishments with unionized nonoffice workers, 1974–1976

Number of employees at establishment	Percent with unionized nonoffice workers
1–49	8
50–99	34
100–499	43
500–999	53
999+	66

Source: Department of Labor survey data, 1974–1976; in Herr, 1989.

Table 7–2. Percentage of employees at different-sized companies and locations who are unionized, 1983

Unit and size	Percent unionized
Company	
Number of employees	
1–24	4
25–99	14
100–499	19
500+	30
Location	
Number of employees	
1–24	7
25–99	20
100–499	29
500+	32

Source: Bureau of Labor Statistics, May 1983 Current Population Survey.

Who Wants Unions?

The unionization rates cited above seem to imply that union representation is more desirable to workers in large firms than to those in small ones. However, this conclusion would be surprising for two reasons. First, to the extent that desire for unionization depends on dissatisfaction with wages and working conditions, the evidence in Chapters 4 to 6 suggests that interest in unions should be strongest among those working for small employers. Second, given that the gap in fringes between large and small employers is smallest in unionized firms, the fringe premium from having a union should be larger if one's employer is small—as, indeed, Richard Freeman and James Medoff (1984) have shown.

How does the desire for unions vary among nonunion employees of different-sized employers? Table 7–3, based on a 1984 Harris survey for the AFL-CIO, sheds light on this question. The first row indicates that the wage-and-salary employees of small nonunion employers are much more likely to say they would vote "union" than comparable employees of large nonunion employers. Row 2 is consistent with these results: among nonunion wage and salary workers, the preference for unions declines significantly with employer size. The third row reveals that when the workers of small employers were given the opportunity to vote in a union

Table 7–3. Union sentiment and activity among private-sector nonunion workers, 1984 (percentages)

Measure	Number of employees in company			Number of employees at location			
	1–99	100–499	500+	1–49	50–99	100–499	500+
1. Would vote "Union"	30	38	24	30	43	28	19
2. Prefer job to be "Union"	21	32	17	23	35	20	13
3. Voted "Union" in election	46	30	33	40	69	30	28
4. Worked where election held	21	19	34	22	23	33	37

Source: Harris survey for the AFL-CIO, 1984, in Medoff, 1987.
Note: Those responding "not sure" were excluded from analysis.

Table 7–4. Union wins per 100 representation elections, by unit size, 1970–1986

Number of employees in unit	1970–1974	1975–1981	1982–1986
1–49	57	52	50
50–99	46	43	41
100–499	42	34	36
500+	38	28	32

Source: NLRB Annual Reports, 1970–1986, in Medoff, 1987, p. 629.

representation election, they were much more likely to have voted for unionization than were the employees of large employers.

Where Do Unions Win?

Evidence on union win percentages in representation elections conducted by the National Labor Relations Board (NLRB) over the past two decades supports the survey data on employee preferences. Table 7–4 indicates that a union's chances of a representation election victory fall sharply and consistently with the size of the unit where organizing is taking place. This difference has remained as the win rate itself has declined.

Unions' recent successes in organizing small employers are particularly striking given that complaints of illegal management opposition to unions are much greater in small units than in those that are large. Table 7–5 indicates that per-employee charges of management unfair practices dur-

Table 7–5. Charges per employee of unfair management
practices in union drives at different-sized units, 1980–1986

Number of employees in unit	Charges per employee
1–49	.23
50–99	.07
100–499	.05
500–999	.07
1000+	.09

Source: NLRB Annual Reports, 1980–1986, in Herr, 1989.

ing union drives were much higher in small units during the 1980–1986 period. Since the vast majority of these charges involved firing for union activity, they are likely to reflect a belief among workers that management is fighting very fiercely. Whether this belief is based on fact or fiction, it is likely to reduce the chances of union success. This reduction can be expected to be larger in small units, where, as we have seen, charges per employee are greater.

Where Do Unions Try?

Despite the fact that among nonunion workers the desire for unionization appears to decline sharply with employer size, unions' organizing efforts appear to grow sharply with size. Among nonunion employees surveyed by Harris in 1984 for the AFL-CIO (see Table 7–3), the respondents of large employers were much more likely to have worked where a union election had been held.

Table 7–6 is quite consistent with the Harris figures. It reveals that in the mid-1970s (comparable data are unavailable for the 1980s), the probability of a union organizing drive appears to have been much higher at large establishments.

Why do unions keep trying to organize big units when it appears they are much more likely to win in small ones? The answer seems simple. Expected revenues from organizing appear to grow much more rapidly with unit size than do expected costs. Dues—hence, revenues—tend to equal about one percent of wages. Given that large units by definition have more workers and that those workers are paid better, expected revenues

Table 7–6. Annual probability of a union election at different-sized establishments, 1974–1976

Number of employees in establishment	Annual election probability
1–49	.02
50–99	.05
100–499	.08
500–999	.07
1000+	.06

Source: Based on figures from the U.S. Labor Department and the National Labor Relations Board, in Herr, 1989.

can grow with unit size even if the chances of a union win do not. On the other hand, it appears that the average cost of organizing does not increase in proportion to the number being organized; thus, organizing cost per potential unit member declines significantly with unit size. Figure 7–1, based on the survey responses of ten union organizers, supports the assertion that organizing costs per potential member are substantially smaller in large units.[1]

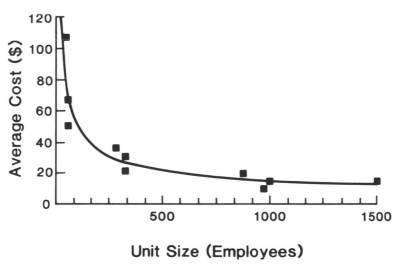

Figure 7–1. Union organizing costs per potential member (*Source*: Survey of ten United Textile organizers nationwide, in Herr, 1989)

·   ·   ·

Those working for large employers are more likely to be unionized than those working for small ones, but among nonunion workers those working for small employers are more likely to want to be unionized. This discrepancy may reflect the fact that unions gain more from organizing larger units. Evidence on the probability of having an election (higher in larger units) and on win rates (higher in smaller units) is consistent with this view. Another factor in the higher unionization rates for large employers may be their greater overall age: not only have they been exposed longer to the possibility of being organized, but also it appears that in the past large nonunion employers did not devote as much effort to preventing unionization as they tend to now. However, small employers today have many characteristics that should make them prime targets for organizing drives.

8

Political Resources

You don't take on small farmers, and you don't take on
small business.

    —David M. Mallino, AFL-CIO lobbyist, 1987

Even in a Congress increasingly awash in contributions from political
action committees (PACs), the activities of the 20,000-member National
Automobile Dealers Association (NADA) stood out. In May 1982 both the
House and Senate voted to veto a rule by the Federal Trade Commission
(FTC) requiring car dealers to place a sticker on auto windshields disclos-
ing known defects and describing the warranties offered. Rhetoric during
the debate ran high. Senate Commerce Committee chairman Bob Pack-
wood said that a veto of the FTC rule would send the public a message
that "we endorse shabby practices. We endorse cheating. We will take no
action against those who would deliberately deceive" (Patterson, 1983,
p. 347). Senator Bob Kasten preferred to portray it as an effort to "use
the legislative veto and other tools that are available to regain control of
the government" (ibid.).

 Although the veto of the FTC used-car rule attracted attention as the
major consumer protection issue considered by Congress that year,
NADA's lobbying actions gave the legislative battle and the outcome even
more limelight. In the 1980 election, NADA's Automobile and Truck Dealers Election Action Committee contributed $1,034,875 toward electing
the Congress that ultimately rejected the FTC rule. According to a Common Cause study, 83 percent of the representatives who voted to kill it
received donations from NADA's PAC (Graves, 1982). In the 1982 elections NADA's PAC contributions of $917,295 made it one of the top ten
PAC contributors to federal-level candidates.

 NADA succeeded in influencing Congress to overrule the FTC, but the
lobby's use of PAC funds did not go unnoticed. As Congressman William
Coyne put it, "In the business of congressional lobbying . . . some are

more clearly equal than others. It is clear to any observer that the arguments of the auto dealers industry have been given greater weight by Congress than those of consumers. The great equalizer is money—especially as it relates to campaign contributions" (Graves, 1982, p. 12). Congressman Thomas Downey declared that what "we have at work here is money influencing political decisions. It embarrasses me" (Patterson, 1982, p. 347). Congressman Toby Moffett stressed the correlation between contributions and votes even more when he declared during the debate: "this ought to not be called the used car rule, but the used Congress rule" (Graves, 1982, p. 12). NADA's PAC-man strategy in fighting the used-car rule became an often-cited example of the power of money to influence congressional votes. The vote also emphasized another reality of Washington politics—the ability of small business to marshal substantial political resources.

Survey data show that the public believes that small business has "too little influence" in politics, in contrast to groups that they view as having too much political power, such as union leaders, corporate executives, and foreign companies operating in the United States (Jackson, 1986).[1] Journalists also view small business as political neophytes. As one article put it: "Politicians love to love small business. The rhetoric is familiar: Small-business owners dare to dream, buck tradition, support their churches, defend freedom and possess faith, intellect, and daring. For politicians, praising small business is like kissing babies—and about as meaningful for those involved" (Jacobs, 1987, p. 41d).

People underestimate the political resources and victories of small business in part because they associate it with fledgling mom-and-pop stores and in part because there is not a single, well-identified voice for small business such as the AFL-CIO for labor. Yet the lobbyists in Washington who represent industries dominated by small businesses (such as NADA, the National Association of Realtors, and the National Association of Home Builders) are rated as among the most effective (Solomon, 1987, p. 1709). This chapter focuses on the resources that small business organizations draw upon in terms of money, staff, votes, and public goodwill; Chapter 9 will examine the impact of small business political power.

Small Business Contributions

Most assessments of the political contributions of small businessmen are summed up in the title of a 1985 article by Steve Coll: "Political Pacmen—

Small Business Money Is Too Meager to Compete for Power and Influence in Washington." The article's predictable message is that contributions from small business PACs are negligible or nonexistent:

> There are only seven PACs that claim to represent small business, according to Federal Election Commission (FEC) records. The combined receipts of all these PACs taken together are roughly equal to the receipts of just one typical Fortune 500 corporation's PAC. Since 1983, small-business PACs collected less than $325,000—loose change compared with the receipts of such leading PAC men as the National Conservative Political Action Committee ($10 million) and the United Auto Workers ($1 million).   (Coll, 1985, p. 22)

Counting only the political contributions of the umbrella groups that represent "small business" ignores the significant contributions by trade groups and professional associations representing the interests of individual industries that are composed primarily of small businesses. Failure to include the money raised by these groups in the total of political funds raised by small business is akin to neglecting the contributions of individual corporate PACs, such as the Tenneco Employees Good Government Fund or the Grumman Political Action Committee, in contributions made by big business because their names do not include specific mention of "big business."

To examine the true extent of the contributions by interest groups in congressional elections, we classified PAC contributions recorded by the Federal Election Commission for House and Senate races from 1978 to 1984 according to whether the money came from groups associated with big business, small business, or labor; the rest of the groups (such as agricultural sectors) were classified as "others" and excluded from analysis. We defined big business funds as those coming from all "corporate" PACs and from trade association PACs for industries in which the majority of employees worked in firms with 500 or more workers.[2] Small business PACs were designated as coming from trade associations or groups representing industries in which the majority of the workers were employed in firms with fewer than 500 people.[3] This definition includes contributions from professional groups such as doctors and lawyers, although in any one year these groups accounted for no more than one-quarter of the small business donations.[4] Labor contributions were defined as those coming from trade union PACs. Varying the definitions of "big" or "small" business industries by using a cutoff number lower than 500 employees does not qualitatively affect our results. Aggregating political contributions in this way does not mean that x dollars are contributed by trade associations to further a single "small business agenda" or that the sum of contributions from individual corporate PACs and large firm trade associations shows support for a monolithic "big business" agenda. Although we will show later that small business trade associations do sometimes work together to promote issues of general interest to small firms, just as individual corporations may work together on issues affecting large firms, it is obvious that many contributions by small business trade associations are given to promote legislation affecting a particular small business industry. Whether the money is given through a trade association PAC representing an individual industry dominated by big or small business (i.e., where the majority of the employees work in firms with more than 500 workers or firms with fewer than 500 workers) or a broader group representing the interests of large or small firms across different industries, an important aspect in judging the total political resources of these interest groups is the total dollars contributed.

The FEC's figures clearly contradict the notion that small business PAC contributions are negligible. Table 8–1 shows that in each election year since 1978, small business PACs contributed nearly two-thirds as much as big business PACs to Senate and House candidates, and roughly the same amount as PACs associated with labor. The relative importance of small business political giving to all candidates is apparent in the 1984 Senate races, where small business provided incumbents and committee chairmen with 23 percent of their total contributions from PACs, and challengers with 11 percent of their PAC funds. The comparable percentages for House candidates in 1984 are 24 percent for incumbents, 19 percent for committee chairmen, and 25 percent for challengers.

Evidence from more recent campaigns confirms the importance of small business contributions in House and Senate races. Of the top ten PAC contributors to federal candidates in 1986, five were from small busi-

Table 8–1. PAC contributions to Senate and House races, 1977–1984 (millions of dollars)

	1977–78	1979–80	1981–82	1983–84
Small business	9.9	15.4	21.4	24.4
Labor	10.4	14.1	21.0	25.5
Big business	11.2	23.3	32.9	39.0

Source: Federal Election Commission data, 1977–1984, in Hamilton and Medoff, 1986.

ness industries: Realtors Political Action Committee, Build PAC of the National Association of Home Builders, American Medical Association PAC, Association of Trial Lawyers PAC, and the National Association of Life Underwriters PAC.

Strength in Numbers

Influencing public policy requires more than financial contributions. It also requires the expenditure of time and effort by trade association and staff members in buttonholing congressional aides, testifying at hearings, and voting in congressional elections. The large organizations that represent the general interests of big business and labor are well known. The AFL-CIO serves as a political coordinator for its 90 international unions, which represent about 70 percent of all American union members. A large part of the AFL-CIO's budget and staff is directed toward lobbying and political activities in elections, efforts that are aided by the federation's Committee on Political Education (COPE) campaign fund. The interests of corporations are similarly represented by groups such as the National Association of Manufacturers (NAM) and the Business Roundtable. NAM, which is perhaps the major employer group in the country engaged in political action involving labor relations, has a national membership of 9,000 manufacturers, an annual budget of $12 million, and a staff of 200. The Business Roundtable, formed in 1972, is an association of the chief executive officers of some of the nation's largest corporations. The Roundtable's prime resource is its ability to mobilize the leaders of the 200 member corporations to lobby Congress and the administration.

Less well known outside Washington but as readily recognized by lobbyists, legislators, and their staff on Capitol Hill are the organizations that represent the interests of small business. Foremost among these is the National Federation of Independent Business (NFIB), a lobbying group with a membership of more than 500,000 businesses, a staff of more than 800, and an annual budget of $40 million. Given the strong incentive of individual small businesses to free ride on the efforts of political groups to which they do not contribute funds, the mere existence of such a large group attests to the strength of the organization. NFIB devotes over half its annual budget to membership recruitment, employing a sales force of 700 representatives who solicit individual businesses to join at dues ranging from $50 to $1,000. In part because small businesses are often short-lived, NFIB must find nearly 100,000 new members every year to maintain its roster (Matlack, 1987). Every sixty days it polls its 500,000 members on five current political issues, sorts the results by zip code, and forwards them to congressional offices; the results also determine which position NFIB will support on a given legislative issue. NFIB mobilizes its most active members into a council that writes letters and visits congressional representatives. In addition, NFIB rates members of Congress according to their voting records on issues of concern to small business, presents Guardian of Small Business awards to those who score at least 70 percent on their issue scorecard, and makes PAC contributions on the basis of these votes.

Other groups also lobby for the interests of small business in Washington. National Small Business United represents about 25,000 businesses and a dozen local and regional small business groups. Foremost among the regional associations is the Smaller Business Association of New England, whose members make a point of talking with individual legislators when they visit their home districts. The U.S. Chamber of Commerce operates a Small Business Center in Washington; its Council of Small Business advises its board on issues of interest to small firms. The degree to which the Chamber actively promotes small business interests, however, is disputed. Although over 90 percent of the Chamber's members are companies with fewer than 100 employees, the lion's share of its budget comes from large corporations, which also hold the majority of seats on the Chamber's board (Richman, 1982a).

Most lobbying in Congress concerns the interests of individual industries rather than battles between "business" and "labor." When individual trade associations in the *Encyclopedia of Associations* are classified according to the same categories we used to study PACs another rough aggregate measure of the political resources of small business emerges.[5] Among the associations listing staff totals, small business associations had approximately 20,000 staff, compared with 15,000 for big business associations and 4,000 for labor unions. These association staffs are particularly valuable in providing information that can influence a legislator's decision or provide a rationale for a decision already reached. Staffs also attempt to influence the form or fate of a bill in hearings before congressional committees. In one major association battle, of the 186 people who testified in hearings on the Labor Law Reform Act of 1977, 40 percent came from unions, 20 percent from small business associations, and 7 percent from groups representing big business. On a less salient issue, of the 38 people who testified on the Equal Access to Justice Act of 1981, which allows a business to recover legal fees from the government if the agency it is involved in a dispute with does not have a "substantially justified position," 66 percent were from small business associations, 5 percent were from big business, and none were from labor organizations.

Although trade associations in industries dominated by small business primarily work to benefit their members through legislation aimed specifically at their industry, they do join together in broader coalitions to work for issues affecting small business in general, just as representatives of large corporations and big business associations conduct joint lobbying campaigns (Lanouette, 1982). The efforts of the 134 trade associations who joined together in the Small Business Legislative Council were highly effective in defeating the Labor Law Reform Act of 1977. During the tax debates of the 1980s, the weekly meetings of the "Big Littles" attracted attention as they brought together small business representatives such as NFIB, the Independent Bankers Association, the Independent Petroleum Association of America, the National Association of Realtors, and others to share information and strategies for lobbying.

When specific legislation would affect a broad class of small business, often temporary coalitions are formed, as when doctors, dentists, optometrists, lawyers, engineers, and accountants lobbied jointly in the early 1980s to restrict the power of the Federal Trade Commission. Likewise, in 1987 business groups united to oppose a package of bills backed by organized labor that would have increased the minimum wage, required companies to offer health insurance and unpaid parental and disability leave, mandated advance notice of large layoffs or shutdowns, and notified employees about exposure to hazardous substances in the workplace (Matlack, 1987). Small business associations organized their members to write letters, make telephone calls, and visit members of Congress; a coalition of trade groups called Concerned Alliance of Responsible Employers (CARE) was formed to lead the opposition to the health insurance and leave bills; and individual associations educated their members about the measures. The National Restaurant Association, for example, briefed more than 200 restaurant owners about to visit Capitol Hill about the benefits legislation and concluded with these instructions: "Explain your position. Relate the issues to your own experience. Try to engage the member in the conversation. Make the sale" (ibid., p. 2592).

Association staff totals understate the lobbying resources of big business, for large corporations are much more likely than small firms to have a Washington office or legislative affairs division. In addition, large corporations can enlist their chief executive officers to carry their message to members of Congress. This in fact is the prime purpose of the Business Roundtable. Explaining the edge that corporation heads have in reaching congressmen, Congressman Willis Gradison of Ohio put it bluntly, "If it's really important to the company, you expect the CEO to get involved. Look, I'm a principal. Principals should talk to principals, staff to staff" (Barry, 1986, p. 28).

Small business has another resource to call upon in legislative battles with big business and labor—a very sizable voting block in every congressional district. The most successful small business associations muster both money *and* constituent votes. Perhaps the most powerful is the National Association of Realtors, which has the largest PAC among the trade associations, raising $4.5 million in 1986. NAR is famous for its ability to turn out realtors to lobby on Capitol Hill. Similarly, such small business groups as the National Association of Life Underwriters and the National Association of Home Builders are skillful at combining contributions (in 1986, $737,317 and $949,772, respectively) with constituent pressure (Solomon, 1987). The Associated General Contractors of America, the chief lobbyist for highway construction firms, clearly demonstrated the power of such pressure by its ability to generate hundreds of telephone calls from its members (most of which are family-owned businesses) during a two-hour period to Senator Terry Sanford, who cast the swing vote to guarantee passage of the highway construction bill in 1987 (ibid.).

Adding to the influence of small business owners is the fact that at the state and congressional levels "small business is big business." Groups such as the U.S. League of Savings Institutions take advantage of the fact that their members, in this case savings and loan executives, are prominent in their communities. As one lobbyist put it, "Even though they're small, they're big in their local communities." He said that when small business owners show up at congressional hearings, "you can see the aides scramble out the back door" to get their bosses to meet with these constituents. Michael Pertschuk, former chairman of the Federal Trade Commission, discovered the power of small business at the local level through the reaction to FTC efforts to restrict anticompetitive practices among the professions and other small businesses. Summarizing his constituents' response, Senator Wendell Ford of Kentucky told Pertschuk, "You have managed to alienate the leading citizens of every town and city in Kentucky: lawyers, doctors, dentists, optometrists, funeral directors, real estate brokers, life insurance companies and salesmen, new and used car dealers, bakers, loan companies, Coca Cola bottlers" (Pertschuk, 1986, p. 41).

Goodwill

A positive public image can also be an asset in swaying legislators. As Table 8–2 clearly demonstrates, small business is viewed much more favorably than big business or labor by the voting public and the press.[6] The results of the three surveys indicate that the public would be much more likely to support programs endorsed by those seen as small business

Table 8–2. The goodwill asset of small business (percentages)

Sample population and question	Response		

1. All adults: "Would you be more or less likely to support a program endorsed by . . . ?"

	More	Less	No difference
U.S. Chamber of Commerce	68	11	21
National Association of Manufacturers	46	16	39
AFL-CIO	46	26	29

2. Journalists: "How would you rate the credibility of the following groups?"

	Good or excellent	
	1982	*1984*
Small business proprietors	71	80
Chief executive officers of corporations	50	53
Public relations executives of corporations	30	37
Labor union leaders	19	14

3. General public and small business owners/managers (1982): "Small businesses should have less government regulation than large businesses."

	Agree	Disagree	Uncertain
General public	67	27	6
Small business owners/managers	75	19	6

Sources: Question 1: Public Interest Opinion Research survey, 1977; question 2: Opinion Research Corporation, 1984; question 3: *Journal of Small Business Management*, 1984.

advocates (68 percent) than programs endorsed by groups representing labor (46 percent) or big business (46 percent). Furthermore, 67 percent of the public agrees with the statement "Small businesses should have less government regulation than large businesses." The table's figures show that journalists rate the credibility of small business much higher than the credibility of big business or labor. Public support for small business can be another resource for the interest group to draw on in lobbying legislators, who themselves are said to view small business as "this idyllic scene of the mom-and-pop shop and isn't it wonderful" (Jacobs, 1987, p. 41d).

A further testament to the goodwill (and constituent vote) assets of small business is the attempts of others to associate themselves with small business in their lobbying campaigns. Part of Chrysler's success in winning federal loan guarantees was attributed to its skillful coordination of the small business contractors (and automobile dealers) who were threatened by the company's collapse (Solomon, 1987). In gaining access to low-interest financing from the Export-Import Bank, Boeing has stressed the gains to its small suppliers and subcontractors (Richman, 1982b). Even intragovernmental lobbying often tries to turn the political resources of small business to advantage. According to one account, when the Department of Defense was threatened by budget reductions, Pentagon officials planned "extensive layoffs of civilian employees and deep cuts in the work of small contractors in an effort to generate a political backlash against Congress for budget cuts" (Halloran, 1987, p. 12).

Small business lobbyists are fortunate to have an underdog image that elicits sympathy from the public and from legislators. But their good fortune does not end simply with a favorable image. Small business industries possess substantial political resources in terms of PAC contributions, associations, and votes. Resources do not necessarily guarantee success, but they do guarantee at least the capacity to influence public policy. The next chapter will examine how this influence affects the working lives of employees in big and small firms.

9

Small Influence

Small business is seen as warm and cuddly. But do they
make a difference? They make a little bit of a difference
on a lot of issues, but there are still too few things on
which they make a big difference.

—Frank S. Swain, Chief Counsel for Advocacy
Small Business Administration, 1987

In Congress, big corporations have nowhere near the
political clout of many groups of small businesses . . .
Far from directing the political currents of our time, big
business will probably be the last to get the word.

—*Wall Street Journal*, 1981

Political resources cannot be equated with political results. Judging the
influence of interest groups by the dollars they spend is like judging successful firms by the amount they spend on advertising. Advertising campaigns vary in their ability to sway consumers; large budgets may be a
sign of a strong product confidently backed or a new product fighting to
gain recognition. Similarly, lobbying campaigns by interest groups vary in
their success in swaying legislators; large contributions may be a sign of
a strong group rewarding its friends or of a weak group fighting to gain
attention. This chapter examines the deployment of one type of political
resource, PAC contributions and their effectiveness as evidenced in
congressional roll-call votes. It also considers the impact of government
policy by examining enforcement of workplace regulations on large and
small employers.

PAC Contributions

The motivations behind PAC contributions are many: a desire to secure
access to legislators; an attempt to ensure the election of friends or the
defeat of opponents; or an effort to influence a legislator's decisions about

an issue through the lure of campaign contributions. Both lobbyists and legislators attest to the pursuit of all three of these strategies of access and influence by small business PACS.

Confirming the importance of maintaining access in Congress, William Hamilton of the NADA PAC relates that "when contributions are made, no demands are made. The contribution says 'we like the way you think and we hope you will open the door to us later'" (Hamilton, 1983, p. 33). Congressman Tony Coelho, an active fundraiser as the chairman of the Democratic Congressional Campaign Committee, described the motives of both givers and receivers more bluntly: individuals giving $5,000 per year or PACs contributing $15,000 to the Speaker's Club he established would gain "access. That's the name of the game. They meet with the Leadership and with the chairmen of committees. We don't sell legislation; we sell the opportunity to be heard" (Drew, 1982, p. 92).

Small business PACs also contribute to influence the outcome of elections so that sympathetic legislators remain in office and those who have opposed their agendas are defeated. This strategy of electoral reward and punishment is most evident in the National Federation of Independent Business's "70-40" rule. NFIB offers potential PAC support to all legislators who score at least 70 percent on its rating of congressional votes of importance to small business, and potential opposition to any legislator who has supported less than 40 percent of those issues.

Evidence for a third PAC strategy, using the lure of campaign contributions to change legislative positions, is often circumstantial. It is usually difficult to tell whether a $1,000 check represents support for an existing position or an inducement to change one. Despite most PACs' claims that their contributions are aimed only at securing access or affecting electoral outcomes, suggestions of outright vote buying sometimes emerge in legislative histories, such as NADA's success in swaying Congress to veto the used-car rule.

Whether PAC contributions are aimed at rewarding friends or at making them, Table 9–1 shows that in the congressional elections from 1978 to 1984 small business PACs contributed generously to those who generally voted for small business positions (as defined by NFIB). Senators and House members who voted the small business line more than half the time received about twice as much small business PAC money per congressman as those who supported small business less consistently. Moreover, because the interests of big business are usually closer to those of small business than to those of labor, the pattern of big business contributions

Table 9–1. PAC contributions and congressional support of small business positions, 1977–1984 (millions of dollars)

PAC contributions per congressman	Senators' support of small business positions		House members' support of small business positions	
	0–50%	51–100%	0–50%	51–100%
Small business	56	140	17	29
Labor	133	52	40	7
Big business	93	290	23	41

Sources: Voting data: National Federation of Independent Business, 1978–1984; PAC contribution data: Federal Election Commission.

Table 9–2. Small business PAC contributions to congressional candidates, 1986

PAC group	Contributions
Industry	
Realtors Political Action Committee	$1,387,429
Build PAC of National Association of Home Builders	949,772
National Association of Life Underwriters PAC	737,317
Dealers Election Action Committee of NADA	419,380
Associated General Contractors PAC	361,814
Independent Insurance Agents of America, Inc., PAC	347,246
Trucking PAC of American Trucking Association	268,045
Professional group	
American Medical Association PAC	869,098
Association of Trial Lawyers PAC	803,600
American Dental PAC	245,625
American Chiropractic Association	153,403

Source: Federal Election Commission release, September 7, 1986.

provides a powerful incentive to support legislation that favors small business. Table 9–2 lists some of the largest "small business" PACs and their contributions to 1986 congressional campaigns. The magnitude of the contributions of a single PAC such as the realtors' shows the importance of the contributions of trade association groups representing small business industries.

The link between contributions and voting is further underscored by the attention that members of Congress devote to their ratings by the nearly seventy organizations that evaluate legislators' support for their positions. The stakes in this rating game are high. Congressman Coelho estimated that an endorsement from the U.S. Chamber of Commerce, an organization that many groups depend upon for information about a congressman's voting record and electoral prospects, can be worth as much as $100,000 in additional contributions. Before the 1980 election several Republican senators lobbied the organization to revise their low voting ratings. The addition of five votes on which the senators had backed the Chamber enabled them to win the group's endorsement (Melia and Phifferling, 1986).

The National Association of Realtors goes beyond simply analyzing roll-call votes; it also requires some candidates seeking money to respond to written questions. In 1982 the group's six-page questionnaire asked for a candidate's position on issues of economic policy that affected realtors and on issues of legislative reform that affected the realtors' lobbying efforts. (One question asked: "Do you agree or disagree that trade associations have a right and responsibility to hold members of Congress accountable for their votes?") Candidates' desire to receive high ratings and the consequent power of lobbying staffs are evident in the comments of the realtors' political resource director, Randall Moorhead, who said in 1982 that in filling out the questionnaire "sometimes candidates plead with me to give them the correct answers" (Isaacson, 1982, p. 23).

The Roll-Call Evidence

Table 9–1 shows clearly that legislators who vote for small business positions receive substantial campaign contributions from small business PACs. However, it is not clear merely from the correlation of contributions and votes that PAC money actually changes the course of legislation. A number of politically plausible theories about PAC contributions do not involve vote buying. A PAC may contribute to candidates it knows favor its position in order to enhance their election prospects. Or a PAC may contribute to candidates because of their general ideology, an ideology that may lead them to support the PAC's positions in the future. A PAC may support the candidates of a given party, whose position in turn lines up with its positions. Or a PAC may contribute to most incumbents simply to assure access.

One way to examine the impact of contributions is to control for the other factors that influence a legislator's votes, such as party, constituents' interests, and ideology. Yet even then a question remains, did the PAC contribute to the campaign because the candidate already favored its position, or did the interest group's contribution sway the representative's vote? Fortunately, political scientists and economists have begun to examine this question by modeling the factors that influence both contributions by PACs and votes by legislators. The simultaneous modeling of both contributions and votes has allowed researchers to address the question of whether, after allowing for the fact that contributions may be given in part because of votes, these contributions actually affect congressional voting patterns.

The evidence to date on PAC contributions in general and on those from small business in particular shows that they do influence votes, though much less than is commonly suggested in coverage of congressional campaign finances. Table 9–3 lists seven PAC studies that have examined contributions from small business groups. The first study confirmed that the higher a legislator's voting rating is on NFIB's congressional scorecard, the higher the probability that he or she will receive an NFIB contribution. The next three studies focused on whether contributions appear to influence votes once other factors such as district interests and a candidate's party and ideology are taken into consideration. For a variety of small business PACs (such as those representing auto dealers, realtors, general contractors, doctors, and truckers), these studies cited in Table 9–3 indicated that contributions do generally have some influence on the votes affecting the economic interests of these groups. The final three studies in the table went one step further and modeled simultaneously the factors that influence contributions and votes. The groups in these studies represented a wide range of small business interests—auto dealers, truckers, savings and loan institutions, home builders, realtors, and doctors. Taking into account both the fact that votes and contributions may influence each other and the other factors that influence the decisions of PACs and legislators, these studies found that contributions do have a small influence on votes in Congress. These results for small business PACs are confirmed in studies of contributions from labor and corporate PACS (Kau et al., 1982; McGaw and McCleary, 1984–85; Owens, 1986; Jones and Keiser, 1987; Saltzman, 1987; Wilhite and Theilmann, 1987).

The story that emerges from these studies is one of marginal influence. Although contributions appear at first glance to have a large effect on votes because of their strong correlation, a deeper examination of the

Table 9–3. Studies associating small business PAC dollars with congressional votes

Study	Small business PAC	Vote	Issue
Poole, Romer, and Rosenthal "The Revealed Preferences of Political Action Committees" (1987)	NFIB	1980, House	NFIB congressional scorecard issues
Welch "The Allocation of Political Monies: Economic Interest Groups" (1980)	Doctors	1974, House	National health insurance (Medicredit)
Frendreis and Waterman "PAC Contributions and Legislative Behavior: Senate Voting on Trucking Deregulation" (1985)	Truckers	1980, Senate	Trucking deregulation
Wright "PACs, Contributions, and Roll Calls: An Organizational Perspective" (1985)	Realtors Auto dealers General contractors Doctors	1981, House 1982, House 1982, House 1982, House	Budget proposal Used-car rules Highway bill FTC regulation
Chappell "Campaign Contributions and Congressional Voting: A Simultaneous Probit-Tobit Model" (1982)	Truckers Auto dealers	1975, House 1977, House	Weight limits Emission standards
Johnson "The Impact of Real Estate Political Action Committees on Congressional Voting and Elections" (1983)	Realtors Doctors Savings and loan Home builders	1978–1980, House 1978–1980, House 1978–1980, House 1978–1980, House	See note
Johnson "The Effectiveness of Savings and Loan Political Action Committees" (1985)	Realtors Doctors Savings and loan Home builders	1978–1980, House 1978–1980, House 1978–1980, House 1978–1980, House	See note

Note: Issues included national park creation, housing and community development, District of Columbia redevelopment, water resources development, agricultural land protection, mortgage bonds, and fair housing.

other factors that might lead legislators to vote for or against a given measure reduces the apparent influence of PAC money on their voting decision. When the fact that votes and contributions simultaneously influence each other is taken into account and examined in models that explore the determinants of both votes and contributions, the impact of contributions is found to be even smaller. But it is present, which indicates that PAC money in general, and small business money in particular in the studies cited in Table 9–3, does influence the outcome of votes of economic concern to interest groups.

The actual influence of small business PAC money may be larger than that found in the studies on congressional roll-call votes. PACs may contribute in part to affect the outcome of elections, so that candidates that favor their positions are more likely to end up in Congress. Work by Gary Jacobson (1980) indicates that spending by challengers increases their probability of election, and trade association PACs (which include small business groups) are more likely than corporate or labor PACs to contribute to challengers' campaigns.

Since Congress at work is Congress in committee, PAC contributions may also influence the fate of legislation at the committee level. One study of contributions to members of the House Committee on Education and Labor found that contributions from business PACs were often given in reaction to those of labor PACs, apparently to offset the influence of opposing interest groups (McGaw and McCleary, 1984–85). PAC money may also have considerable influence on issues with less visibility (Jones and Keiser, 1987). Given that many small business issues do not attract a great deal of media attention, the influence of small business contributions on the less visible issues such as small business exemptions tucked away in major legislation or dealt with in committee may mean that the real impact of small business funds is greater than that on roll-call votes alone.

Another way to measure the impact of the political resources marshaled by small business would be to estimate the value of the subsidies and regulatory exemptions enjoyed by small business industries. Such a task, however, is beyond the scope of this study for at least three reasons. First, given the large number of small business industries aided and protected by the government, we would have to evaluate an enormous amount of government policy. Second, determining whether these subsidies were large relative to those for labor and big business would involve an even larger round of calculations. Finally, examining such a large number of disparate government policies would take us far afield from our prime focus, the working lives of people in large and small firms. We have chosen instead to focus on one aspect of government policy, namely regulatory enforcement, to see how outcomes in this area affect the workers of large and small employers.

Enforcement of Regulations

A common moral in many regulatory horror stories is that federal regulations hit small businesses harder than larger ones. This message often accompanies the assertion that small and large businesses are subject to the same regulatory restraints. It is also assumed that because there is often a fixed cost in complying with a regulation, small businesses are at a disadvantage because they sell fewer units over which to spread the costs of compliance.[1] These concerns about the effects of regulation focus on owners' profits and the survival of the business, with little attention to the effects of regulatory differences on the workers in big and small firms.

Small and large firms are not subject to the same regulatory restraints. Small firms and establishments enjoy regulatory exemptions in a wide array of federal programs both from explicit standards written in the law (*de jure*) and from the manner in which the rules are enforced (de facto). In their study of the scope of these exemptions in *The Economics of Small Businesses*, William Brock and David Evans have noted:

> The Toxic Substances Control Act of 1976 exempts small chemical companies from various testing and reporting requirements. The Office of Federal Contract Compliance exempts businesses with fewer than fifty employees from filing affirmative action plans. The Occupational Safety and Health Administration exempts firms with fewer than twenty employees from routine inspections. The civil penalties assessed by the Environmental Protection Agency under the Federal Insecticide, Fungicide, and Rodenticide Act vary with firm size. Larger firms are assessed larger penalties than smaller firms for comparable violations. The Securities and Exchange Commission tiers reporting requirements for security issues according to the size of the issue.   (Brock and Evans, 1986, p. 74)

As of 1981 the U.S. Regulatory Council had identified forty-three regulatory programs whose compliance and reporting requirements varied with the size of the business. As of 1982, the EPA had tiered almost fifty different regulations on the basis of firm size or amount of pollutant released (SBA, 1983). Such exemptions may even have increased since then as a result of the Regulatory Flexibility Act of 1980, which encourages agencies to use methods such as the scaling of regulatory requirements to avoid burdening small businesses disproportionately. The populist inclination to favor small institutions is evident in the fact that the Regulatory Flexibility Act covers not only small businesses but also small public institutions such as colleges and small municipalities.[2]

Evidence is more mixed on the claim that regulatory compliance costs small businesses more than it does large ones. Estimates of this inequity abound, such as the finding by a report for the Federal Home Loan Bank Board that regulatory costs to savings and loan institutions with assets of less than $10 million were thirteen times as high per million dollars of assets as those of their counterparts with $100–200 million in assets (Brock and Evans, 1986, p. 132). Bartel and Thomas (1985, 1987) conclude that OSHA regulations disproportionately affect the profits of small firms. Similarly, the Small Business Administration estimates that "paperwork burdens alone cost small business $12.7 billion per year" (ibid., p. 103).

The argument that regulatory compliance costs are relatively higher for small firms is intuitive. If complying with a federal rule such as one limiting the release of air pollutants requires purchasing a given technology, the small firm may have fewer units of sales over which to spread the fixed costs of the technology. Its cost disadvantage will cause it to lose sales and perhaps even go out of business. In the long run, the effect of the regulation may be to change the distribution of firm size within the industry so that smaller firms are less likely to survive. Thus, in the two years following passage of the 1969 Coal Mine Health and Safety Act, one-third of the more than 400 coal producers in West Virginia that employed fewer than fifteen people went out of business (Neumann and Nelson, 1982). Yet is this an isolated incident or symbolic of the general burdens of regulation?

In the most comprehensive survey of the impact of regulations on small business, Brock and Evans concluded that "there is no credible evidence that environmental or health and safety regulations have had a widespread disparate impact on smaller manufacturing plants. The statistical results . . . do not enable us to reject the hypothesis that regulations have had a neutral impact across plant sizes and that there are no scale economies in regulatory compliance" (1986, p. 136). They do find that some regulations affect small businesses more heavily because they are more likely to engage in the prohibited practices. Thus,

> The mattress flammability standard, coal mine safety regulation, and Davis-Bacon Act have had a disparate impact on smaller businesses because these businesses were more likely to be engaging in the behavior policy makers wished to discourage. Small mattress producers were producing more flammable mattresses, small coal mines had higher accident rates, and small construction companies relied more heavily on cheap, nonunion labor than did larger businesses in the respective industries. In these cases, the regulation itself rather than scale economies in regulatory compliance had a disparate impact on small businesses. (1986, p. 136)

What is the impact of the degree of regulatory enforcement in small firms on their workers? Focusing on the regulations that affect the working life of employees, our research indicates that under the system of *de jure* and de facto regulatory exemptions enjoyed by small businesses, workers in these firms appear to enjoy less regulatory protection than their counterparts who work in large businesses.

Evidence compiled across many industries in a study by David Weil (1987) indicates that enforcement of health and safety regulations may indeed be more lax in small firms. As Table 9–4 shows, the probability of inspection for compliance with the Occupational Safety and Health Act (OSHA) (1974) rises dramatically with firm size, whether the establishment is in construction, manufacturing, or services. Weil's figures also indicate that large unionized establishments are much more likely to be inspected than their nonunion counterparts, in part because unions act as

Table 9–4. OSHA inspection probabilities in different-sized union and nonunion establishments, by sector, 1985

Number of employees at establishment	Construction		Manufacturing		Services	
	Union	Nonunion	Union	Nonunion	Union	Nonunion
Less than 100	.17	.13	.06	.14	.002	.002
100–249	.36	.13	.37	.22	.05	.01
250–499	.40	.12	.51	.19	.14	.03
500 or more	1.00	.36	.95	.16	.77	.06

Source: Weil, 1987, pp. 228–230.
Note: The closer the number is to 1.00, the greater the chance of being inspected.

advocates in inviting inspections. Because of the heavy concentration of employment of small firms in small establishments, these workers are left uncovered by de facto exemptions that favor small establishments.

Weil found a similar pattern of more vigilant inspection in larger workplaces in the implementation of the Mine Safety and Health Act of 1969. Table 9–5 reveals that inspections per year increased with mine size in both periods examined, and that this pattern again was even stronger for unionized mines. In addition, Weil found that larger companies in the underground coal industry paid heavier fines per ton of coal produced than did their smaller counterparts with similar working conditions. In terms of OSHA enforcement in manufacturing firms, companies with 500 or more employees paid substantially more in fines per affected worker for each violation of safety and health standards than did smaller firms with similar working environments, industry characteristics, and union status.

Small firms' experience with regulations governing minimum wage and overtime pay often generate stories about the long arm of the government, such as the *Wall Street Journal* report that began:

> When the Labor Department inspector pays a visit, business owners can be hurt—especially by what they don't know. Ivan and Jean Cooper, who own and operate Ye Olde Ironmaster and Sir Beef Ltd., two small restaurants in Reading, Pennsylvania, have learned that lesson from bitter, firsthand experience. In a compliance case brought against them in 1979 that's still pending, the Labor Department contends the Coopers must pay $6,000 in back wages to employees. It also says the couple owes another $6,800 in federal fines for violating minimum wage, overtime and child-labor regulations. (James, 1982)

Although such experiences involve genuine burdens on the owners involved, evidence from the Minimum Wage Study Commission on com-

Table 9–5. Coal mine inspections, by size of mine, 1981–1983

Number of tons produced annually	Average number of employees, 1982	1981–1982		1982–1983	
		Union	Nonunion	Union	Nonunion
0–29,999	11	21	11	21	10
30,000–99,999	20	16	16	17	18
100,000–499,999	79	32	20	35	22
500,000+	325	79	53	83	53

Source: Weil, 1987, pp. 127, 137.

pliance nationwide suggests that violations of minimum wage and overtime laws are much more common in small workplaces than in large ones
(Sellekaerts and Welch, 1981). Table 9–6 shows that a higher percentage
of workers in smaller establishments are likely to be paid in violation of
overtime provisions. The commission also found that if a minimum wage
violation does occur it is more likely to affect a higher percentage of the
workforce in smaller establishments and that the vast majority of workers
who are not paid according to minimum wage standards work in small
establishments.[3]

Aside from differences in the *enforcement* of regulations, explicit
exemptions for small firms result in less protection for workers there than
for their counterparts in larger firms. A clear example is the exemption of
small firms from the monitoring system set up by the Equal Employment
Opportunity Commission. All firms with 100 or more employees and federal contractors with $50,000 in contracts and with 50 or more employees
must file an annual report listing their total employment by race and sex
for different occupational categories. These reports can form the basis for
detection of hiring discrimination. Largely as a result of exemptions for
small firms, fewer than half of all private sector workers outside of education are covered by these reports (Smith and Welch, 1986). Although in
theory employers who are exempt from simple reporting requirements
might still hire in the same manner as others, James Smith and Finis Welch
(1986) find that minority employment has expanded much more rapidly in
firms that are subject to EEOC reporting than in those that are not.

Further exemptions for small firms from labor regulations continue to
be debated. In the 100th Congress, an exemption for businesses with

Table 9–6. Percentage of employees in different-sized locations
paid in violation of overtime provisions of the Fair Labor
Standards Act, 1979

Number of employees at location	Percent paid in violation of overtime provisions
1–19	13
20–99	6
100–499	2
500–999	3
1000+	0

Source: Tabulations of Minimum Wage Study Commission Noncompliance Survey, 1979, in Sellekaerts and Welch, 1981, pp. 108–109.

fewer than 15 employees was included in a bill requiring employers to offer unpaid leaves with job protection for family reasons (such as births or adoptions) or serious illness, although nearly one-quarter of the private workforce works in firms with fewer than 15 employees (Rovner, 1987). Measures to require employers to offer health insurance provisions included exemptions for small business. The controversial proposal to require a company to give sixty days' notice before closing a plant also tiered its regulations: companies with fewer than 100 employees or laying off fewer than 50 workers would be exempt, as would firms laying off less than one-third of their workforce, unless more than 500 workers were involved (Blinder, 1988). These exemptions were included despite complaints from union leaders that plant closings in smaller firms were particularly troublesome because these firms rarely gave as much advance notice as larger firms (*Wall Street Journal*, June 3, 1987, p. 1).

The regulatory exemptions for small business arise in part because small business lobbyists argue that they cannot afford to meet the same requirements as larger firms. Commenting on the proposed legislation requiring health plans and parental leave, the president of NFIB John Sloan observes, "You can't have a fringe benefit until you have a job" (Mellon, 1987, p. 37). He says that in the process of small business job creation, "we're talking about marginal employers picking up some marginal employees, all of which feeds this system positively. And you start heaping this on [mandating benefits] and start eliminating tens of thousands of jobs, the net effect on us all is drag." Efforts to raise the minimum wage have also run aground on opposition from small businessmen. As one congressman asked in the 1988 debate on the issue, "Who does this bill really help? We've got to think about the little businessman as well as the little working man" (Morehouse, 1988, p. 1013).

Debate about the proper scope of regulations affecting small and big firms will undoubtedly continue, especially as new evidence becomes available about regulatory costs. What is clear today, however, is that two workers in the same industry but in different-sized firms may face different work environments because *de jure* or de facto regulatory exemptions offer the employee in the smaller firm less protection. This pattern may emerge because of small business lobbying, efforts by regulators to economize on enforcement costs by targeting larger firms, or a belief that regulations unduly burden small firms. The question that should be asked more frequently in discussions of regulatory exemptions is, "Do we really want to be a country with two workforces, one protected and the other not?"

· 10 ·

A Fuller Picture

Few areas in our national life are as important to our economic health and well-being as small business. Small enterprises represent the economic backbone of communities across the country, the major source of job creation in the United States, and a vital source of the innovation, new products, and services which drive our economy . . . Far from a national abstraction, small business to each of us represents the very heart of economic opportunity in America and a linchpin of our social and economic cohesion.

—Jimmy Carter and Gerald Ford, 1985

The picture that emerges from our research differs from popular conceptions about big and small business. Part of this difference stems from actual disagreements about the economic and political roles played by small employers. Part of the difference also stems from our emphasis on facts often overlooked about the total package offered to workers by large employers. Recasting the images of large and small employers is not simply an exercise in academic debate, however. These images often form the backdrop for public policy debates whose outcomes may differ depending on whether workers are employed by large or small firms.

We have seen that small employers do not create a strikingly large share of jobs in the economy, especially if we count only jobs that are not short-lived. Most jobs are generated by new firms, which happen to be small; existing small firms have relatively high chances of failing, and when this failure rate is taken into account, they do not grow faster than larger firms. Indeed, in recent years they have shrunk, and faster than large firms. The share of employment accounted for by small firms has been remarkably constant.

The kinds of jobs generated vary significantly by employer size, a point often overlooked in job generation discussions. Workers in large firms earn higher wages, and this fact cannot be explained completely by differences in labor quality, industry, working conditions, or union status. Workers in large firms also enjoy better benefits and greater job security than their counterparts in small firms. When these factors are added together, it appears that workers in large firms do have a superior employment package. The higher quit rates and greater desire for unionization in small firms provide additional evidence on the quality of jobs offered by large employers.

We have seen that in terms of campaign contributions, association staff, and public goodwill, the political resources of small business are substantial. We have also seen that in terms of regulatory enforcement, the system of *de jure* and de facto exemptions for small firms leaves their workers with less protection than their counterparts in large firms. Finally, we have seen that to the extent that government policy favors the interests of small business owners, the direction of income redistribution will be from the bottom to the top since small business owners enjoy incomes and assets greater than those of the average American.

The idea that small business enjoys support because of its job generation capability was clear in David Birch's 1981 article:

> We know very little about who the major job creators are, where they are active, who controls those jobs, and who is most likely to respond to changes in economic policy. In the absence of such knowledge, national policy has been to stimulate the entire economy as though it acted as a single unit, using instruments like broad tax incentives, easier access to money, and public works programs of various sorts. This can be a very expensive and inflationary approach if, in fact, most of the recipients do not use the incentives to increase employment and productivity. What we need, and have lacked, is the ability to focus our incentives on those who will make good use of them without wasting taxpayers' monies on those who will not.   (p. 4)

Birch's conclusion that small business creates the most jobs was transformed by policymakers, especially at the state level, into a belief that small business creates nearly all jobs. Programs to fund and nurture small firms proliferated in the 1980s; by 1988 forty-three states had adopted programs to aid small businesses and were providing an estimated $700 million per year in startup financing for them (Pae, 1988). Throughout this period small business advocates linked support for their programs with their role in job creation.

The early claims of small business job generation were clearly oversold.

The true proportion of jobs generated by smaller firms is closer to their actual share of the workforce, especially when the shorter life of small business jobs is taken into account; but the "eight out of ten" myth lingers on. Programs based on this myth may be successful, and they may even have been supported by legislators on grounds other than their job generation ability. But to the extent that support for programs is based on the belief that small firms should be nurtured because they are generators of a disproportionately large number of long-lived U.S. jobs, it is misguided.

More fundamentally, however, the share of new jobs created by small firms is a statistic in search of a compelling policy implication. The case for tilting the playing field to the advantage of small business must rest on what an *extra* billion dollars of encouragement will do, and the share of new jobs generated by small firms at present does not tell us anything about the impact of such incentives. Indeed, a big business advocate could argue that the "disproportionate" job creation of small businesses is a sure sign that they have already received disproportionate help in the form of regulatory exemptions or government contract set-asides.

While the case for favoring small business is frequently oversold, one can go too far in righting the balance of public discussion. Small firms do appear to contribute more than their share of innovations, and they provide more than their share of opportunities to young, inexperienced workers. And they do face real disadvantages: they pay more when they borrow money, and more when they buy supplies. They fail frequently. But they do not necessarily fail as a result of costs associated with regulatory compliance.

Whether exemptions for small firms are granted in order to reduce their burden of compliance costs or to reduce the costs of enforcement, the effect is to worsen an already much inferior work environment. Employees in small firms have lower wages, fewer fringes, and less job security. Exemptions from Equal Employment Opportunity laws, laxer enforcement of occupational safety and health regulations, and similar exemptions result in less regulatory protection for workers in small businesses. Tailoring regulations to different-sized workplaces involves a difficult balancing act among jobs, workers, and owners. Concern for the growth of small business should be weighed against concern for the protection of the workforce. Providing an exemption for firms with fewer than 100 employees leaves one-third of all American workers unprotected; an exemption for workplaces with fewer than 100 employees leaves half of the workforce unprotected (SBA, 1986a, pp. 11, 30). The tradeoffs between worker protection and economic viability in government regulations affecting small businesses should be explicit and based on facts, not on populist sentiment. Sentiment aside, the results of our research suggest a clear message for policies affecting large and small firms: Do not judge employers by their size alone.

Notes

References

Index

Notes

1. Images of Large and Small Employers

1. Ross (1984, 1986) provides extensive discussion of attempts by small retailers to fight the growth of chain stores through legislation.

2. The Economic Backdrop

1. These figures come from revised estimates from the SBA (telephone interview with SBA staff, July 1988). Small firms' share of sales is measured in terms of "gross product originating," which is defined as the part of gross national product generated by private business using resources resident within the country.
2. See SBA (1983, 1987) for a review of small businesses' role in innovation.

3. Generating New Jobs

1. The calculations in the text are only approximate, because they miss the creation of multiple-establishment firms. However, these are likely to be very minor (Phillips and Kirchhoff, 1988). In any case, they stack the deck slightly against the point we are making—by missing a small number of new, multiple-establishment firms we are underestimating the importance of firm births in the job generation process.
2. Leonard (1986) argues that the faster growth rates of small firms are a statistical illusion: small firms are disproportionately likely to be firms that have shrunk recently, and they seem to "grow" disproportionately when this temporary shrinking is reversed. Hall (1987) finds no evidence of such "regression to the mean" in her data. The difference between the two studies (which use different data sets, both of which in any case underrepresent really small firms) has not been resolved.

4. Wages

1. Using longitudinal data for young men, Evans and Leighton (1989) find that those who change employers earn more if they move to larger employers rather than to

smaller ones. This difference, however, is not statistically significant when they exclude those working for firms with fewer than 25 workers.

2. Dunn (1980, 1984) tried to assess the disutility of work by comparing the number of dollars workers would pay for (hypothetical) fringe benefits with the number of unpaid hours they would work to obtain the same fringes. She found that this disutility rose with firm size in one sample but not in the other; even in the first sample, the wage premium more than offset the increased disutility. Her results are therefore consistent with our finding that, taken together, variations in working conditions are at best a partial explanation for the size-wage relationship.

3. For a cogent discussion of this idea, see Bulow and Summers (1986).

4. See Brown and Medoff (1989) for a more detailed discussion of the analysis of the size-wage premium among piece-rate workers.

5. For a discussion of this matter see, e.g., Masters (1969) and Mellow (1982).

6. For a more detailed discussion of each table see Brown and Medoff (1988), which also contains evidence on discounts for nonfuel inputs and finds the fuel discounts representative of those on the broader set of inputs.

5. Who Benefits?

1. Further evidence supporting the SBA finding that large firms offer more in the way of fringe benefits comes from ICF (1987), table 2–2, which shows that large firms' expenditures on voluntary fringe benefits are a much higher percentage of the payroll than in small firms.

6. The Total Package

1. Economists sometimes infer the amount of training from the rate at which earnings rise on the job. This approach is risky, because employers may pay higher wages to workers with more seniority for other reasons besides their becoming more productive (e.g., because of seniority provisions in contracts or as a reward for satisfactory performance to that point). In any case, evidence here too is mixed: studies of worker-reported data tend to find earnings rising faster at large firms; but the professional, administrative, technical, and clerical pay data described in Chapter 4 suggest that the size of the premium falls as employees move to higher pay grades.

2. Quit rates are generally lower for those with more schooling and experience and may also be lower for those who are "better" in unmeasured ways. Since large employers hire better workers, our inability to hold constant all dimensions of worker quality could lead us to overestimate the effect of employer size on quits. By holding the wage constant, however, we should also indirectly hold constant unmeasured worker quality (which raises wages).

7. Employer Size and Unions

1. Another reason to concentrate on larger units is the fact that they have lower closing rates, as discussed in Chapter 3.

8. Political Resources

1. This evidence may mean that the public believes that small business owners lack the resources to influence policy, or that the public believes that small business owners should have more influence because they support these entrepreneurs, or both.
2. All contributions listed as "corporate" by the FEC are treated as coming from big business, even though not all corporations contributing PAC dollars are large in terms of number of employees.
3. Information on employee distribution by firm size is from the Small Business Administration's four-digit Standard Industrial Classification (SIC) code data base on firm size and employment in 1984 (SBA, 1986b).
4. Inclusion of the professions in the small business category may seem to go against the association of lawyers with corporations and of doctors with medical companies. Yet many of the lobbying efforts of these associations relate to restricting entry to the professions, in a manner similar to other small businesses' attempts to protect their markets. Eighty-nine percent of those who work in law firms work in companies with fewer than 500 people, while 91 percent of those who work in the medical field work for firms with fewer than 500 employees (SBA, 1986b).
5. Association staff totals are from the *Encyclopedia of Associations, 1987.* The classification system used is the same one employed for categorizing PAC donations. Our classification system does not capture how well an individual industry's association represents the interests of big firms versus small firms in the industry.
6. In sample question 1 of Table 8–2 we assume that perceptions equate the U.S. Chamber of Commerce with small business interests, the National Association of Manufacturers with big business, and the AFL-CIO with labor.

9. Small Influence

1. This section draws upon Brock and Evans's (1986) excellent summary of the research on the effect of regulation on small businesses.
2. McGartland (1984) found that sources of pollution from municipalities and very small businesses were less heavily regulated and that this pattern of regulation increased the cost of the pollution reduction achieved by the EPA.
3. The Minimum Wage Study Commission did take into account the statutory exemptions from some regulations for establishments that did not meet a certain threshold of sales.

References

Acs, Zolton, and David Audretsch. 1988. "Innovation in Large and Small Firms: An Empirical Analysis." *American Economic Review* 78 (September): 678–690.

Adams, Walter, and James W. Brock. 1987. "Corporate Size and the Bailout Factor." *Journal of Economic Issues* 21 (March): 61–85.

Andrews, Emily. 1989. *Pension Policy and Small Employers: At What Price Coverage?* Washington, D.C.: Employee Benefit Research Institute.

Armington, Catherine, and Marjorie Odle. 1982. "Small Business: How Many Jobs?" *Brookings Review* 20 (Winter): 14–17.

Bandow, Doug. 1986. "A Corporate Lobby Pulls Its Punches." *Wall Street Journal*, July 23, p. 20.

Barron, John M., and John H. Bishop. 1985. "Employer Search—The Interviewing and Hiring of New Employees." *Review of Economic Statistics* 67 (February): 43–52.

Barron, John M., Dan A. Black, and Mark A. Lowenstein. 1987. "Employer Size: The Implications for Search, Training, Capital Investment, Starting Wages, and Wage Growth." *Journal of Labor Economics* 5 (January): 76–89.

Barry, John M. 1986. "CEOs Make the Best Lobbyists." *Dun's Business Month*, January, p. 127.

Bartel, Ann P., and Lacy Glenn Thomas. 1985. "Direct and Indirect Effects of Regulation: A New Look at OSHA's Impact." *Journal of Law and Economics* 28 (April): 23–25.

—— 1987. "Predation through Regulation: Wage and Profit Effects of the Occupational Safety and Health Administration and Environmental Protections Agency." *Journal of Law and Economics* 30 (October): 239–261.

"Big Is Powerless." 1981. *Wall Street Journal*, September 8, p. 34.

Birch, David L. 1981. "Who Creates Jobs?" *Public Interest* 65 (Fall): 3–14.

—— 1987. *Job Generation in America*. New York: Free Press.

Bishop, John H. 1982. "The Social Payoff for Occupationally Specific Training: The Employers' Point of View." Technical report for National Center for Research in Vocational Education, Ohio State University.

References · 100

—— 1985. "The Magnitude and Determinance of On-the-Job Training." In *Training and Human Capital Formation*, ed. John Bishop, Kevin Hollenbeck, Suk Kang, and Richard Willhe. Columbus: National Center for Research in Vocational Education, Ohio State University.

Blinder, Alan S. 1988. "Plant Closings: It Pays to Give Workers Advance Notice." *Business Week*, June 6, p. 19.

Bluestone, Barry, and Bennett Harrison. 1982. *The Deindustrialization of America*. New York: Basic Books.

Bowes, Marianne, Frank P. R. Brechling, and Louis S. Jacobson. 1985. *Unemployment Insurance and Firm Size*. Alexandria, Va.: Center for Naval Analyses.

Brock, William A., and David S. Evans. 1986. *The Economics of Small Business: Their Role and Regulation in the U.S. Economy*. New York: Holmes and Meier.

Brown, Charles, and James Medoff, 1988. "Cheaper by the Dozen." Mimeograph. Harvard University.

—— 1989. "The Employer Size Wage Effect." *Journal of Political Economy* 97 (October): 1027–59.

Bulow, Jeremy, and Lawrence Summers. 1986. "A Theory of Dual Labor Markets, with Applications to Industrial Policy, Discrimination, and Keynesian Unemployment." *Journal of Labor Economics* 4 (July): 376–414.

Bureau of Labor Statistics, U.S. Department of Labor. 1940. *Hourly Earnings of Employees in Large and Small Enterprises*. Washington, D.C.: U.S. Government Printing Office.

—— 1974 (May), 1979 (May), 1983 (May). Data tape for Current Population Survey. Washington, D.C.

Chappell, Henry, Jr. 1982. "Campaign Contributions and Congressional Voting: A Simultaneous Probit-Tobit Model." *Review of Economics and Statistics* 64 (February): 77–83.

Chelius, James R., and Robert S. Smith. 1985. *Workers Compensation Costs by Firm Size*. Alexandria, Va.: Center for Naval Analyses.

Chilton, Kenneth W. 1984. "What Should Government Do for Small Business?" *Journal of Small Business Management*, January, pp. 1–3.

Cohen, Wesley M., Richard C. Levin, and David C. Mowery. 1987. "Firm Size and R&D Intensity: A Reexamination." *Journal of Industrial Economics* 35 (June): 543–565.

Coll, Steve. 1985. "Political Pacmen—Small Business Money Is Too Meager to Compete for Power and Influence in Washington." *INC.*, August, p. 22.

Converse, Muriel, Richard Coe, Mary Corcoran, Maureen Kallick, and James Morgan. 1981. "The Minimum Wage: An Employer Survey." In U.S. Minimum Wage Study Commission, *Report*. Vol. 6. Washington D.C.: U.S. Government Printing Office. Pp. 241–341.

Couretas, John. 1985. "Small Business Innovation Research Programs, Federal Help for the Little Guy's High-Tech R&D." *Business Marketing*, August, p. 74.

Curtin, Edward. 1970. *White Collar Unionization*. New York: National Industrial Conference Board.

Curtin, Richard F., Thomas Juster, and James N. Morgan. Forthcoming. "Survey

Estimates of Wealth: An Assessment of Quality." In *The Measurement of Saving, Investment, and Wealth*, ed. Robert E. Lipsey and Helen S. Tice. Chicago: University of Chicago Press.

Drew, Elizabeth. 1982. "Politics and Money—Part One." *New Yorker*, December 6, pp. 57–58.

Dunn, Lucia. 1980. "The Effects of Firm and Plant Size on Employee Well-Being." In *The Economics of Firm Size, Market Structure, and Social Performance*, ed. John Siegfried. Washington, D.C.: Federal Trade Commission.

—— 1984. "The Effects of Firm Size on Wages, Fringe Benefits, and Worker Disutility." In *The Impact of the Modern Corporation*, ed. Harvey Goldschmid et al. New York: Columbia University Press.

Dunne, Timothy, and Mark Roberts. 1987. "The Duration of Employment Opportunities in U.S. Manufacturing." Mimeograph. Pennsylvania State University.

Dunne, Timothy, Mark Roberts, and Larry Samuelson. 1987. "Plant Turnover and Gross Employment Flows in the U.S. Manufacturing Sector." Mimeograph. Pennsylvania State University.

—— 1988. "The Growth and Failure of U.S. Manufacturing Plants." Mimeograph. Pennsylvania State University.

Encyclopedia of Associations. 1987. Detroit: Gale Research.

Evans, David S., and Linda S. Leighton. 1987. "Why Do Smaller Firms Pay Less?" Manuscript. Fordham University.

—— 1989. "Why Do Smaller Firms Pay Less?" *Journal of Human Resources* 24 (Spring): 299–318.

Foulkes, Fred. 1982. *Personnel Policies in Large Nonunion Companies*. Englewood Cliffs, N.J.: Prentice-Hall.

Freeman, Richard B., and James L. Medoff. 1984. *What Do Unions Do?* New York: Basic Books.

Frendreis, John P., and Richard W. Waterman. 1985. "PAC Contributions and Legislative Behavior: Senate Voting on Trucking Deregulation." *Social Science Quarterly*, 66 (June): 401–412.

Garen, J. 1985. "Worker Heterogeneity, Job Screening, and Firm Size." *Journal of Political Economy* 93 (August): 715–739.

Goldin, Claudia. 1986. "Monitoring Costs and Occupational Segregation by Sex: A Historical Analysis." *Journal of Labor Economics* 4:1–27.

Graves, Florence, ed. 1982. "PAC Spending: Getting Bigger All the Time." *Common Cause* 8 (August): 26–27.

Greene, Richard. 1986. "Can You Handle Chaos?" *Forbes*, June 16, pp. 156–157.

Haber, Sheldon. 1988. "Participation in Industrial Training Programs." Survey of Income and Program Participation working paper 8813. U.S. Census Bureau, Washington, D.C.

Hall, Brownyn. 1987. "The Relationship between Firm Size and Firm Growth in the U.S. Manufacturing Sector." *Journal of Industrial Economics* 35 (June): 583–606.

Halloran, Richard. 1987. "Pentagon Plans to Lay Off Civilians as It Cuts Budget." *New York Times*, October 25, p. 20.

Hamermesh, Daniel. 1980. "Commentary" (on papers by J. Kwoka and F. Stafford). In *The Economics of Firm Size, Market Structure, and Social Performance*, ed. John Siegfried. Washington, D.C.: Federal Trade Commission.

Hamilton, James T. 1983. "PACing the U.S. Senate in 1980: An Econometric Study of the Contributions of Political Action Committees." Honors thesis, Harvard College.

Hamilton, James T., and James L. Medoff. 1986. "Small Is Powerful: The Political Resources and Victories of Small Business." Mimeograph. Harvard University.

Harris and Associates, 1984. Data tape for the AFL-CIO Union Image Survey. New York, NY.

Hartman, Curtis. 1985. "The Spirit of Independence." *INC.*, July, pp. 46–50.

Herr, John. 1989. "Union Organizing Behavior and Establishment Size." Honors thesis, Harvard College.

Hill, Elizabeth. 1987. "Post-Secondary Vocational Training in Pennsylvania—In School and on the Job." Mimeograph. Pennsylvania State University at Mont Alto.

—— 1988. "Effects of Postsecondary Technical Education on the Job." Manuscript. Pennsylvania State University at Mont Alto.

Holzer, Harry, Lawrence Katz, and Alan Krueger. 1988. "Job Queues and Wages: New Evidence on the Minimum Wage and Inter-Industry Wage Structure." NBER Working Paper 2561. Cambridge, Mass.

ICF Incorporated. 1987. "Health Care Coverage and Costs in Small and Large Businesses." Report prepared for Office of Advocacy, Small Business Administration. Washington, D.C.

Isaacson, Walter. 1982. "Running with the PACs." *Time*, October, pp. 20–24.

Jackson, John E. 1986. "The Climate for Entrepreneurial and Small Business." Mimeograph. University of Michigan.

Jacobs, Sanford L. 1987. "The Multibillion Dollar Weakling." *Wall Street Journal*, May 15, p. 41d.

Jacobson, Gary. 1980. *Money in Congressional Elections*. New Haven: Yale University Press.

James, Frank. 1982. "A Couple's Bitter Experience When Labor Inspector Visits." *Wall Street Journal*, August 9, p. 15.

Johnson, Linda. 1983. "The Impact of Real Estate Political Action Committees on Congressional Voting and Elections." *AREUEA Journal* 11:462–475.

—— 1985. "The Effectiveness of Savings and Loan Political Action Committees." *Public Choice* 47:289–304.

Jones, Woodrow, Jr., and K. Robert Keiser. 1987. "Issue Visibility and the Effects of PAC Money." *Social Science Quarterly* 68 (March): 170–176.

Kau, James, et al. 1982. "A General Equilibrium Model of Congressional Voting." *Quarterly Journal of Economics* 97 (May): 271–293.

Koek, Karin E., Susan B. Martin, and Annette Novallo, eds. 1989. *Encyclopedia of Associations*. Detroit: Gale Research.

Kozmetsky, George, Robert A. Peterson, and Nancy M. Ridgway. 1984. "Opinions about Government Regulation of Small Business." *Journal of Small Business Management*, January, pp. 56–62.

Kruse, Douglas. 1989. "Supervision, Working Conditions, and the Employer Size-Wage Effect: An Empirical Analysis." Mimeograph. Rutgers University.

Lanouette, William. 1982. "Off the Hill and Off the Record, Lobbyist Clubs Dine on Gourmet Tips." *National Journal*, April 10, pp. 630–634.

—— 1988. "Reel Heroes Think Small." *Best of Business Quarterly*, Summer, p. 73.

Leonard, Jonathan. 1986. "On the Size Distribution of Employment and Establishments." NBER Working Paper 1951. Cambridge, Mass.

Lester, Richard. 1967. "Pay Differentials by Size of Establishment." *Industrial Relations* 7 (October): 57–67.

Levitt, Arthur, Jr. 1981. "In Praise of Small Business." *New York Times Magazine*, December 6, p. 136.

Lipset, Seymour M., and William Schneider. 1987. *The Confidence Gap: Business, Labor, and Government in the Public Mind*. Baltimore: Johns Hopkins University Press.

Lublin, Joann S. 1984. "Development Aid from States is a Growing Factor for Firms." *Wall Street Journal*, October 8, p. 33.

Masson, Robert, and P. David Qualls, eds. 1976. *Essays in Industrial Organization in Honor of Joe S. Bain*. Cambridge, Mass.: Ballinger.

Masters, Stanley. 1969. "An Interindustry Analysis of Wages and Plant Size." *Review of Economics and Statistics* 51 (August): 341–345.

Matlack, Carol. 1987. "Mobilizing a Multitude." *National Journal*, October 17, pp. 2592–96.

McCraw, Thomas K. 1984. *Prophets of Regulation*. Cambridge, Mass.: Harvard University Press.

McGartland, Albert M. 1984. "Marketable Permit Systems for Air Pollution Control: An Empirical Study." Ph.D. diss., University of Maryland.

McGaw, Dickinson, and Richard McCleary. 1984–85. "PAC Spending, Electioneering and Lobbying: A Vector ARIMA Time Series Analysis." *Polity* 17:574–585.

Medoff, James L. 1979. "Layoffs and Alternatives under Trade Unions in U.S. Manufacturing." *American Economic Review* 69 (June): 380–395.

—— 1987. "The Public's Image of Labor and Labor's Response." *Detroit College of Law Review*, Fall, pp. 609–636.

Melia, Thomas, and Sueanne Phifferling. 1986. "Heroes and Zeroes." *New Republic*, October 27, p. 8.

Mellon, George. 1987. "Small Firms Brace for a Legislative Attack." *Wall Street Journal*, May 5, p. 37.

Mellow, Wesley. 1982. "Employer Size and Wages." *Review of Economics and Statistics* 64 (August): 495–501.

Morehouse, Macon. 1988. "Bill to Boost Minimum Wage Faces Rough Sailing in House." *Congressional Quarterly*, April 16, pp. 1012–13.

Nader, Ralph, and William Taylor. 1986. *The Big Boys*. New York: Pantheon Books.

National Commission on Jobs and Small Business. 1987. *Making America Work Again: Jobs, Small Business, and International Challenge*. Washington, D.C.

National Federation of Independent Business. 1978–79 through 1984. *How Congress Voted, 95th Congress through 98th Congress*. Washington, D.C.

NBC News. 1988. Poll Results 143, February 5.

Neumann, George R., and Jon P. Nelson. 1982. "Safety Regulation and Firm Size Effects of the Coal Mine Health and Safety Act of 1969." *Journal of Law and Economics* 25 (October): 183–199.

Oi, Walter. 1983. "Heterogeneous Firms and the Organization of Production." *Economic Inquiry* 21 (April): 147–171.

Oi, Walter, and John Raisian. 1985. "Impact of Firm Size on Wages and Work." Mimeograph. University of Rochester, Rochester, New York.

Opinion Research Corporation, Opinion Research Survey. 1984. Princeton, N.J.

Osborne, David. 1988. *Laboratories of Democracy*. Boston: Harvard Business School Press.

Owens, John E. 1986. "The Impact of Campaign Contributions on Legislative Outcomes in Congress: Evidence from a House Committee." *Political Studies* 34 (June): 285–295.

Pae, Peter. 1988. "Start-up Companies Find States Becoming Their Biggest Boosters." *Wall Street Journal*, January 13, p. B2.

Pakes, Ariel, and Richard Ericson. 1989. "Empirical Implications of Alternative Models of Firm Dynamics." NBER Working Paper 2893. Cambridge, Mass.

Pappas, Vasil J., ed. 1987. "How Will You Fare in the 'New Economy'?" In *Managing Your Career (Wall Street Journal* circular).

Patterson, Eugene, ed. 1983. *1982 Congressional Quarterly Almanac*. Washington, D.C.: Congressional Quarterly.

Pear, Robert. 1987. "U.S. to Focus on Major Companies on Curb of Aliens." *New York Times*, April 24, p. 413.

Pertschuk, Michael. 1986. *Giant Killers*. New York: Norton.

Phillips, Bruce, and Bruce Kirchhoff. 1988. "Analysis of New Firm Survival and Growth." Paper presented at Babson Entrepreneurship Research Conference. Office of Advocacy, Small Business Administration, Washington, D.C.

Poole, Keith T., Thomas Romer, and Howard Rosenthal. 1987. "The Revealed Preferences of Political Action Committees." *American Economic Review* 77 (May): 208–302.

Popkin, Joel, and Company. 1987. "Small Business Gross Product Originating 1958–82." Report prepared for Small Business Administration. (SBA 1040-OA-86). Washington, D.C.

Posner, Richard A. 1981. *Antitrust Cases, Economic Notes, and Other Materials*. St. Paul, Minn.: West Publishing.

Pound, Edward T. 1988. "Pentagon Payoffs: Honored Employee Is a Key in Huge Fraud in Defense Purchasing." *Wall Street Journal*, March 2, p. 1.

Powers, Ron. 1987. "Reel Villains." *Best of Business Quarterly*, Summer, pp. 71–74. Reprinted from December 1987 issue of *Business Month*.

Prescott, Edward, and Michael Visscher. 1980. "Organizational Capital." *Journal of Political Economy* 88 (June): 446–461.

Pugel, Thomas. 1980. "Profitability, Concentration, and the Interindustry Variation in Wages." *Review of Economics and Statistics* 62 (May): 248–253.

Rees, Albert, and George Shultz. 1970. *Workers and Wages in an Urban Labor Market*. Chicago: University of Chicago Press.

Richman, Tom. 1982a. "Can the U.S. Chamber Learn to Think Small?" *INC.*, February, pp. 82–86.

—— 1982b. "Will the Real Small Businessman Stand Up?" *INC.*, July, pp. 26–28.

—— 1983. "What America Needs Is a Few Good Failures." *INC.*, September, pp. 63–72.

Rosen, Sherwin. 1982. "Authority, Control, and the Distribution of Earnings." *Bell Journal of Economics* 13 (Autumn): 311–323.

Ross, Thomas W. 1984. "Winners and Losers under the Robinson-Patman Act." *Journal of Law and Economics* 27 (October): 243–271.

—— 1986. "Store Wars: The Chain Tax Movement." *Journal of Law and Economics* 29 (April): 125–137.

Rovner, Julie. 1987. "'Family Leave' Bill Moves Forward in House." *Congressional Quarterly*, May 16, p. 999.

Saltzman, Gregory M. 1987. "Congressional Voting on Labor Issues: The Role of PACs." *Industrial and Labor Relations Review*, January, pp. 163–179.

Scherer, F. M. 1976. "Industrial Structure, Scale Economies, and Worker Alienation." In *Essays on Industrial Organization in Honor of Joe S. Bain*, ed. Robert Masson and P. David Qualls. Cambridge, Mass.: Ballinger.

—— 1980. *Industrial Market Structure and Economic Performance*. Boston: Houghton Mifflin.

Schiller, Bradley R. 1983. "'Corporate Kidnap' of the Small-business Employee." *Public Interest* 72 (Summer): 72–87.

Scott, Oscar E. 1984. *Small Business and the 98th Congress*. CRS report IB84015. Washington, D.C.: Congressional Research Service, Library of Congress.

Sellekaerts, Brigitte, and Stephen Welch. 1981. "Violations of the Fair Labor Standards Act: Inferences from the 1979 Noncompliance Survey." In U.S. Minimum Wage Study Commission, *Report*, Vol. 3. Washington, D.C.: U.S. Government Printing Office. Pp. 77–113.

Siegfried, John, ed. 1980. *The Economics of Firm Size, Market Structure, and Social Performance*. Washington, D.C.: Federal Trade Commission.

Small Business Administration. 1982 through 1985, 1986a, 1987, 1988a. *The State of Small Business: A Report of the President, 1982* through *1988*. Washington, D.C.

—— 1986b. "1984 Firm Employment and Sales: 4-Digit SIC." Database, August 21. Computer printout. Washington, D.C.

—— 1988b. Tabulations on job growth. Washington, D.C.

"Small Business in America." 1986. Advertising supplement, *U.S. News and World Report*, August 21.

Smart, Tim. 1985. "The Take at the Top." *INC.*, September, pp. 67–74.

Smith, James P., and Finis R. Welch. 1986. *Closing the Gap: Forty Years of Economic Progress for Blacks*. Santa Monica, Calif.: Rand.

Solomon, Burt. 1987. "Measuring Clout." *National Journal*, July 4, pp. 1706–11.

Solomon, Steven. 1986. *Small Business USA: The Role of Small Companies in Sparking America's Economic Transformation*. New York: Crown.

"A Special News Report on People and Their Jobs in Offices, Fields and Factories." 1988. *Wall Street Journal*, June 2, p. 1.

Stafford, Frank. 1980. "Firm Size, Workplace Public Goods, and Worker Welfare." In *The Economics of Firm Size, Market Structure, and Social Performance*, ed. John Siegfried. Washington, D.C.: Federal Trade Commission.

Stewart, Milton D. 1982. "Public Enemy Number One: With All the Talk about Deficits, We've Lost Sight of the Fact That Jobs Are the Key to a Healthy Economy." *INC.*, April, p. 128.

Stigler, George. 1962. "Information in the Labor Market." *Journal of Political Economy* 70:94–105.

Stolzenberg, Ross M. 1978. "Bringing the Boss Back In: Employer Size, Employee Schooling, and Socioeconomic Achievement." *American Sociological Review* 43 (September): 813–828.

Survey Research Center, 1973, 1977. Data tape for Quality of Employment Survey. University of Michigan.

Swain, Frank S. 1988. "The Economic Impact of the HIV Epidemic on Small Business." Statement before the Presidential Commission on Human Immunodeficiency Virus Epidemic, May 10.

United States Census Bureau. 1982. Data tape for Census of Manufacturers. Washington, D.C.

Weil, David. 1987. "Government and Labor at the Workplace: The Role of Labor Unions in the Implementation of Federal Health and Safety Policy." Ph.D. diss., Harvard University.

Weiss, Andrew, and Henry Landau. 1984. "Wages, Hiring Standards, and Firm Size." *Journal of Labor Economics* 2 (October): 477–499.

Weiss, Leonard. 1966. "Concentration and Labor Earnings." *American Economic Review* 56 (March): 96–117.

Welch, W. P. 1980. "The Allocation of Political Monies: Economics Interest Groups." *Public Choice* 35:97–120.

"Who Loves You More? A Debate between Partisans." 1983. *INC.*, June, p. 19.

Wilhite, Allen, and John Theilmann. 1987. "Labor PAC Contributions and Labor Legislation: A Simultaneous Logit Approach." *Public Choice* 53:267–276.

Wojahn, Ellen. 1984a. "Beyond the Fringes: How Smaller Companies are Profiting from Flexible-benefits Plans." *INC.*, July , pp. 106–109.

—— 1984b. "How to Cut $5,000 off the Cost of Each Employee." *INC.*, July, pp. 106–109.

—— 1984c. "The Take at the Top." *INC.*, September, pp. 44–56.

Woodbury, Stephen A. 1983. "Substitution between Wage and Nonwage Benefits." *American Economic Review* 73 (March): 166–182.

Wright, John R. 1985. "PACs, Contributions, and Roll Calls: An Organizational Perspective." *American Political Science Review* 79:400–414.

Index